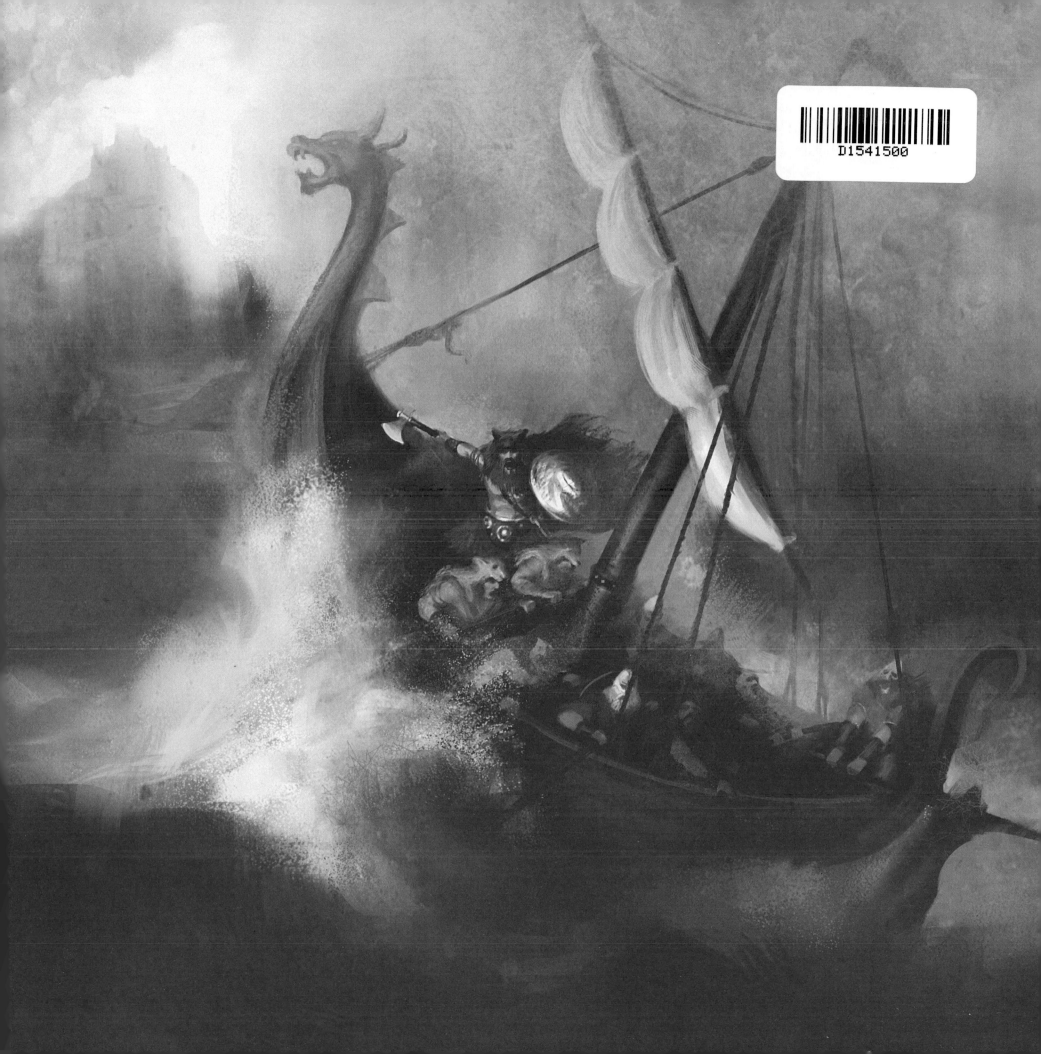

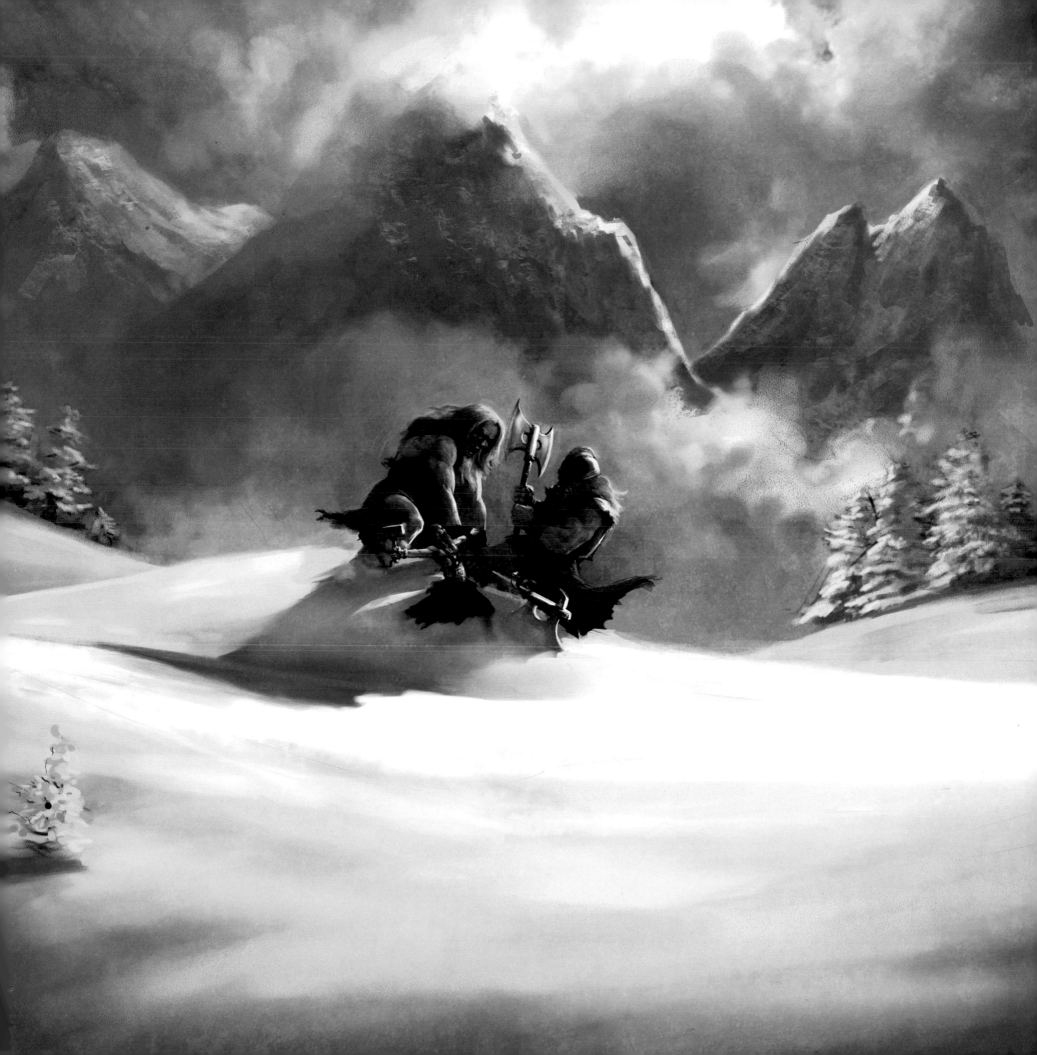

Lost Worlds

Vikings

The creators of this book would like to express their sincere thanks to:

Dr. R.W. Dance at the Department of Anglo-Saxon, Norse and Celtic
at Cambridge Universty for his help with the entry regarding the
Anglo-Saxon Chronicle

Frank Frazetta for providing the inspiration to the illustration on page 1; this
illustration was based on his painting *The Frost Giants' Daughter*

Peter Tunstall and Northvegr.org for the translation of the *Saga of Ingvar the
Far-traveled* inside page 52

Árni Magnússon Institute in Iceland for the use of the
manuscript SAM 66 on page 75

Published by Sterling Publishing Co., Inc.
387 Park Avenue South, New York, NY 10016

© **2007 Flat Planet Media Limited**
Written by J.M. Clements
Designed by Allen Boe
Edited by Royce Meyer
Illustrations pp. 1, 23, 33, 51, 69, 99, 115 by Marc Simonetti
Illustrations pp. Inside front cover, 12, 15, 16, 19, 24, 27, 31, 35, 36, 37, 38,
40, 44, 45, 47, 52, 62, 67, 73, 74, 79, 81, 83, 89, 92, 98, 99, 106, 108, 115,
119, 125, 127, 132 by Miguel Coimbra
Additional illustrations by Allen Boe and Dover Publications

Distributed in Canada by Sterling Publishing
c/o Canadian Manda Group, 165 Dufferin Street,
Toronto, Ontario, Canada M6K 3H6

Distributed in the United Kingdom by GMC Distribution Services,
Castle Place, 166 High Street, Lewes, East Sussex, England BN7 1XU

Distributed in Australia by Capricorn Link (Australia) Pty. Ltd.
P.O. Box 704, Windsor, NSW 2756, Australia

ISBN-13: 978-1-4027-5218-6
ISBN-10: 1-4027-5218-0

Printed in China

2 4 6 8 10 9 7 5 3 1

For information about custom editions, special sales, premium and
corporate purchases, please contact Sterling Special Sales
Department at 800-805-5489 or specialsales@sterlingpub.com.

Lost Worlds

Vikings

J.M. Clements

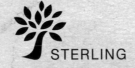

STERLING

New York / London
www.sterlingpublishing.com

CONTENTS

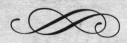
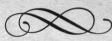

✪ INTRODUCTION ✪

The End of the World

"In this year there were immense flashes of lightning, and fiery dragons in the air, and a little after that the raiding of heathen men destroyed God's church in Lindisfarne."

—Anglo-Saxon Chronicle

On June 7, A.D. 793, a group of violent criminals landed on the Holy Isle of Lindisfarne off the northwest coast of Britain. Without warning, they attacked the monastery, snatching priceless Christian artifacts for their value in precious metals.

8

"And they came to the church of Lindisfarne, laid everything waste with grievous plundering, trampled the holy places with polluted feet, dug up the altars and seized all the treasures of the holy church. They killed some of the brothers; some they took away with them in fetters; many they drove out, naked and loaded with insults; and some they drowned in the sea."

—Simeon of Durham

heathen men destroyed God's church

Right: A page from the Anglo-Saxon Chronicle

B
rittene igland is ehta hund mila lang.
⁊ twa hund brad. ⁊ her sind on þis
iglande fif ge þeode. englisc ⁊ brit
tisc. ⁊ wilsc. ⁊ scyttisc. ⁊ pyhtisc. ⁊
boc leden. Erest weron bugend þises
landes brittes. þa coman of armenia. ⁊ ge setan
suðewearde bryttene ærost. Þa ge lamp hit þ pyh
tas coman suþan of scithian. mid langū scipū
na manegū. ⁊ þa coman ærost on norþ ybernian
up. ⁊ þer bædo scottas þ hi ðer moston wunian. ac
hi noldan heom lyfan. forðan hi cwædon þa scottas.
we eow magon þeah hwaðere ræd ge læron. we witan
oþer igland her be eastan. þer ge magon eardian gif
ge willað. ⁊ gif hwa eow wið stent. we eow fultumiað. þ
ge hit magon ge gangan. Ða ferdon þa pihtas. ⁊ ge
ferdon þis land norþan weard. ⁊ suþan weard hit hæf
don bryttas. swa we ær cwedon. And þa pyhtas heom abæ
don wif æt scottum. on þa ge rad þ hi ge curon heora
kyne cin aa on þa wif healfa. þ hi heoldon swa lange
syððan. ⁊ þa ge lamp hit ymbe geara runa. þ scotta
sum dæl ge wat of ybernian on bryttene. ⁊ þes lan
des sum dæl ge eodon. ⁊ wes heora heretoga reoda ge
haten. from þa heo sind ge nemnode dæl reodi. Six.
tigum wintrū ær þe crist were acenned. gai iuli
romana kasere mid hund ehtatigū scipū ge sohte
bryttene. Þer he wes ærost ge swenced mid grimmum
ge feohte. ⁊ micelne dæl his heres for lædde. ⁊ þa he

As news spread of the event, the Christian world was shocked beyond belief. Nobody would have dreamed of attacking a church or monastery—the very idea would be thought of as a hellish crime. Now, no coastal community could regard itself as safe. Far to the south in what is now Germany, the terrified Anglo-Saxon monk Alcuin summed up the terror of the Christian community, which had believed itself to be safe from harm:

> *"It is some 350 years that we and our forefathers have inhabited this lovely land, and never before in Britain has such a terror appeared as this we have now suffered at the hands of the heathen. Nor was it thought possible that such an inroad from the sea could be made."*

Alcuin went further, suggesting that this was not merely an act of vicious criminals, but a sign predicted in the Bible of the approaching end of the world:

> *"Then the Lord said unto me, Out of the North an evil shall break forth upon all the inhabitants of the land…"*
>
> *—Jeremiah, 1:14*

10

For the next two hundred years, all Europe would shiver in fear at the approach of the terrifying Northmen, soon known by a more famous name… the **VIKINGS!**

out of the north an evil shall break forth

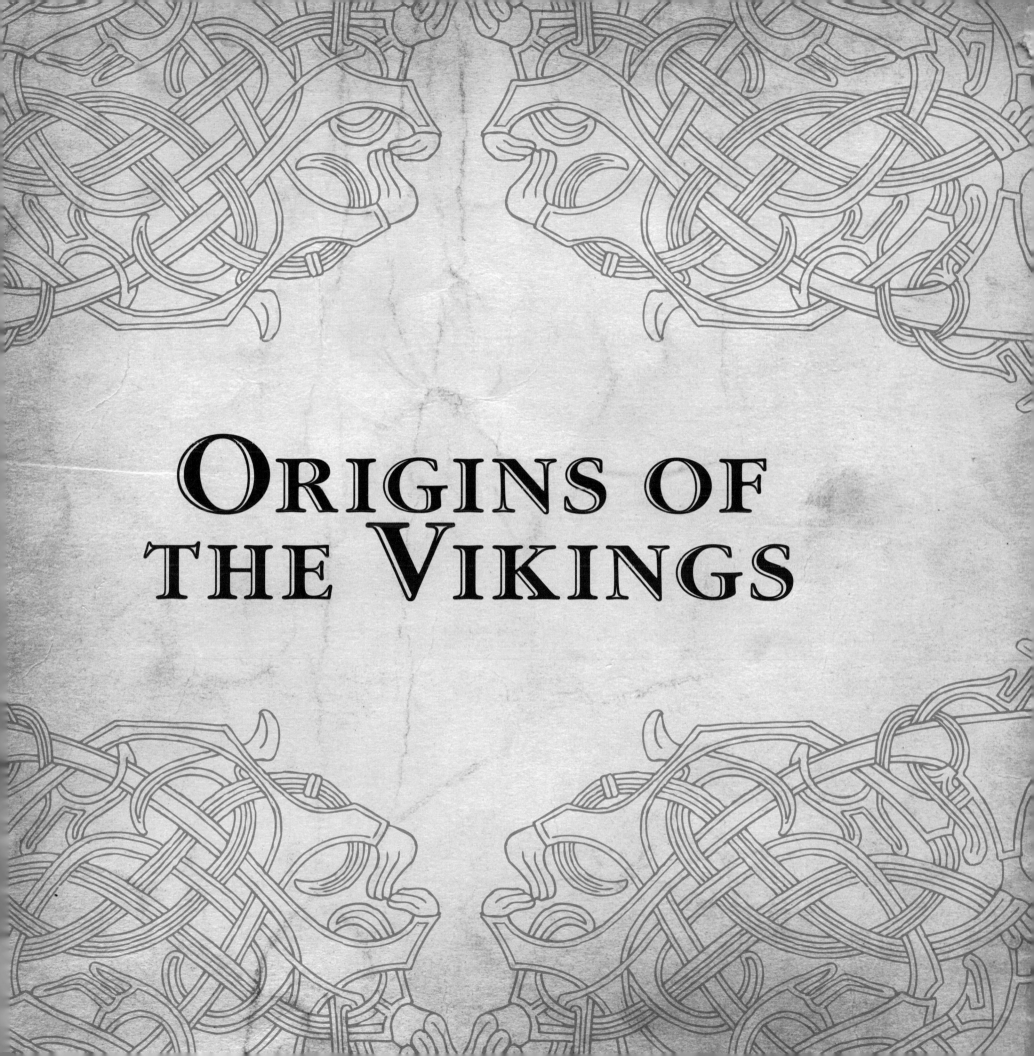

Origins of the Vikings

A Surprise Attack?

Our information about the first Viking raids comes from an unreliable source—the Vikings' victims at Lindisfarne and their sympathizers. The shock and terror of the first accounts ignores other evidence that suggests the Viking Age did not begin on that fateful day in 793, but well before that.

It is unlikely that the men who attacked Lindisfarne had sailed directly across the sea from Scandinavia, the Viking homeland. They had probably been in the region of the British Isles for some time, perhaps first as traders, before deals turned sour, money dried up, and they turned to crime. Before the attack on Lindisfarne, Scandinavians had even been trendsetters in the north of England, where local men had adopted their braided hairstyle to show how tough they were. Archaeologists in Scotland have uncovered the ruins of a village completely destroyed by unknown raiders—just like Lindisfarne.

12

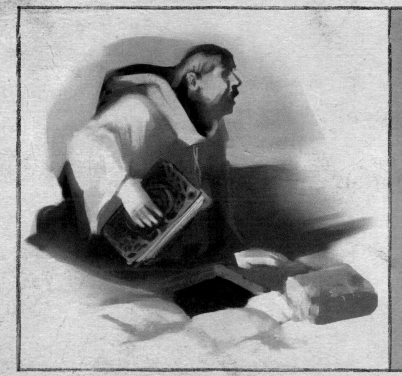

Without Warning?

Despite the surprise attack, the monks of Lindisfarne must have had enough warning of the attack to hide or spirit away their most treasured possessions, such as the Lindisfarne Gospels. Vikings did not care for Christian books, but would happily smash the ornate covers and hinges to use them as brooches, and pry jewels out of settings in these sacred objects.

Right: An example of the artistry in the Lindisfarne Gospels

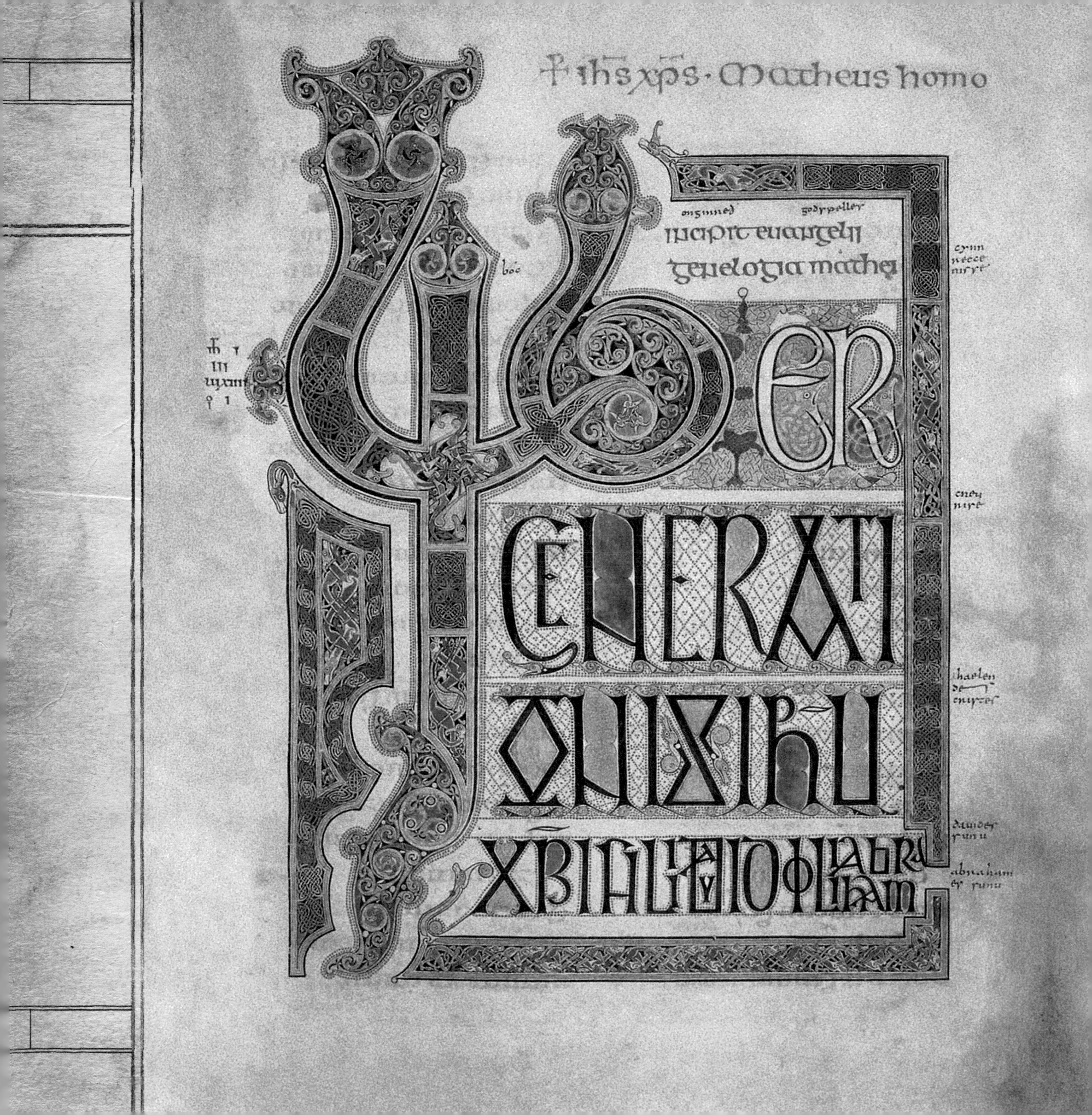

† ihs xps · Mattheus homo

on ginned   godspelles
incipit euangelii
genelogia matthei   boc

LIbER
GENERATI
ONISIHU
XBIFILIIDAUIDFILIIABRAHAM

Signs of Trouble

Four years before the attack on Lindisfarne, there was a report of a strange incident in Portland, in the south of what is now England, when the Norwegian crews of three ships attempted to land without permission and killed a local law enforcer. Three years later, King Offa of Mercia ordered the construction of sea defenses. Do his actions imply earlier, unrecorded attacks? Whether they do or not, Mercia's coasts remained safe for a time, while the Vikings raided Northumbria and Scotland.

Before long the raiders were back; monasteries and communities on the coasts of England, Ireland, and Wales reported further attacks.

Phantom Raiders?

It is likely that there were many more Viking attacks in the period, but no survivors were left to report them. The Vikings took not only valuables, but also slaves, and it is possible that entire villages simply disappeared.

14

A Prayer for Salvation

Summa pia gratia nostra conservando corpora et custodita, de gente fera Normannica nos libera, quae nostra vastat, Deus, regna.

(Oh great and holy grace, protecting us and ours, deliver us, oh lord from the fierce tribe of Northmen who lay waste to our realm!")

This prayer was used in the dedication of churches to the saints Vaast and Medard in the aftermath of the raid on Lindisfarne.

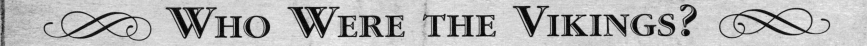

Who Were the Vikings?

The Vikings are generally acknowledged to be the warriors who left Scandinavia in the years between 793-1066 to trade and raid all across Europe. Where they found "empty" ground, such as in the Faeroe Islands or Iceland, they settled and often became peaceful farmers. Where they met with strong resistance, as in the Byzantine Empire, they backed off. But where pickings were rich, they returned again and again to rob the local inhabitants, either by carrying off treasures and slaves, or by demanding "tribute" —bribes to stay away.

The precise origin of the name "Viking" is buried in the past. A *vík*, in Old Norse, was a bay or inlet, while *víkja* was swift movement. Some connection with these terms led to the new words *viking* (a pirate raid) and *víkingr* (a pirate raider).

No Country

There is no such place as "Vikingland." Vikings are not a race or a nationality—the name describes a profession. Although the majority of them came from the Scandinavian region, there are mentions in the sagas of "Vikings" from Poland, Germany, Scotland and Wales.

15

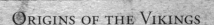

Other Countries, Other Names

NAME	MEANING	SOURCE
Wicingas kynn	Kin of the Pirates	Old English poem
Normanni	Northmen	Latin (in France)
Gall	Strangers	Irish chronicles
Dani	Danes	English chronicles
Varangoi	Pledgers	Greek military
Al-Waranke	Pledgers	Arabic corruption of the Greek
Al-Majus	Heathens	Arabic (in Spain)
Ascomanni	Ash-men	German (ships of ash wood)
Rootsi	Rowers	Estonian reports
Rusioi	Blonds/Ruddy	Greek chronicles
Ar-Rus	Blonds/Ruddy	Arabic corruption of the Greek

16

The "Viking age" saw scattered bands of warriors leaving Scandinavia in search of fortunes abroad, and eventually returning to carve out kingdoms for themselves in their native lands. It ended when the pagan Vikings were largely converted to Christianity. Much of the aggression of the Vikings was thereafter directed away from Christendom towards new enemies—on a series of Crusades against "heathens" in northeastern Europe or Muslims in the Holy Land.

THE HOMELAND OF THE VIKINGS

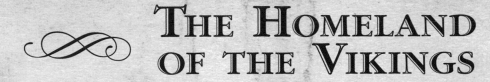
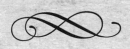

The vast majority of the men known to Europeans as Vikings came from Scandinavia. Although it comprises Europe's northernmost point, parts of Scandinavia can be surprisingly warm, thanks largely to the Gulf Stream that gives Norway wet but mild summers.

Norway

Modern-day Scandinavia is divided into three countries. The area now known as Norway was originally the "North Way"—a long chain of islands and sheltered harbors running all the way up the west coast of Scandinavia that protected local ships from the worst storms of the Norwegian Sea.

Flat land in Norway suitable for farming is limited to two areas: the region around modern Trondheim and the region around modern Oslo. Both areas produced Norway's earliest kings and earliest rivals. Deep, narrow inlets, or fjords, lead inland from the sea, while steep mountains occupy much of the interior. It was thus relatively easy to go from coastal town to coastal town by ship, and perilously difficult to do so by land, encouraging the early Norwegians to become seafarers.

A vast mountain range stretches all the way from north to south in Norway, cutting it off from Sweden to the east. The people of Viking time called this range the Keel, which translates as "waste."

Waste Land?

Despite Viking legends to the contrary, the Keel was not waste land at all. It was home to numerous tribes of Saami people—reindeer herders who dwelled far to the south along the upland ranges. The Vikings called them Finns, confusing them with other tribes to the east in Finland. They were also often known as Lapps—a derogatory name derived either from patches of clothing worn by the poor, or from the Finnish lape, meaning "periphery."

Although the Saami were a different race than the Vikings, their languages share many words, implying prolonged contact. Saami appear in Viking sagas as priests, shamans, and beautiful witches, and they may have functioned in a religious context among some Viking bands. They were said to have the power to summon breezes to fill sails, and the ability to leave their bodies as scouts in the spirit world.

17

Sweden

The area now known as Sweden sits to the east of the Keel, and included similar mountain areas and dense forests. It favored a shipbuilding culture; traveling between homesteads was much easier when undertaken by boat, and Sweden's traders soon learned to sail the relatively calm waters of the Baltic Sea, in search of markets in Finland, Poland, and other Baltic countries. Some of the trade hardly warranted the description, and was instead described as collection of tribute. The most heavily populated area of Sweden in the Viking Age was the area around modern Stockholm, which stands on the coast where the long Lake Mälaren reaches deep into the Swedish hinterland.

Iceland

The Vikings settled in many places, but the relative isolation of Iceland allowed its colonists to cling much more strongly to their Scandinavian roots. The remote island of Iceland became a colony and a refuge for the Vikings, and the place where many of their histories and legends were preserved.

18

Directions

Future Viking expeditions often reflected the geographical outlook of the Vikings' places of origin. Norwegians tended to sail out into the wide sea, first as fishermen, then as traders, then as raiders and settlers in the Shetland Islands, the Orkney Islands, the Faeroes, and then Britain, Ireland, Iceland, and beyond. Danes followed similar routes, but also clung to the coastline of mainland Europe, raiding in France and Spain, and trading eastward into the Baltic. Swedes concentrated on the Baltic and the river system leading down into Russia and the Black Sea.

Denmark

Although the bulk of modern Denmark's land mass is the Jutland Peninsula that projects from Germany, the region also includes several large islands, making sea transport as important to the ancient Danes as to the other Scandinavians.

BEFORE THE VIKINGS

Human beings came late to Scandinavia, settling around 8,000 years ago as the last Ice Age finally receded from northern Europe. Scattered farmsteads eked out an existence, particularly in Denmark and southern Sweden, where there was marginally more land. The locals were using bronze by 2000 B.C. and iron by 500 B.C.

The inhabitants of Scandinavia already were known as sea-rovers long before the Viking Age began. Roman accounts list conflicts with ship-borne raiders from Scandinavia, while back in the sailors' homeland, fortified bases such as those at Eketorp on Öland, or Gamla Uppsala in Sweden, point to local rulers imposing their authority on small areas.

Just before the dawn of the Viking Age, in the Vendel period (A.D. 600-800), the Scandinavians displayed signs of an advanced culture. Local notables were buried in their ships, and society in Denmark was organized enough to build a defensive wall on its southern border.

19

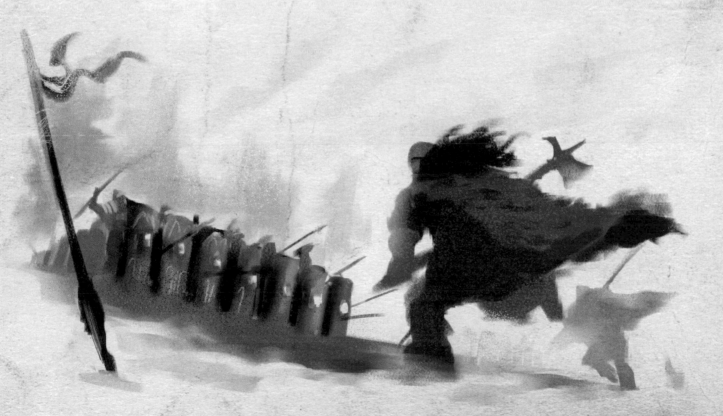

The Great Wall of Denmark

It is said that there was not one but many kings of Denmark before the Viking Age. Regardless, the legendary King Godfred was powerful enough to command the construction of the Danevirke ("Dane-work"), an earthen wall between 11.5 to 19.5 feet tall that stretched across the south end of the Jutland Peninsula. A road ran along the northern coast, allowing friendly merchants to offload their cargoes on the North Sea side, and carry them across to the Baltic Sea in relative safety. Dendrochronology has dated the construction of the Danevirke to three phases between 737 and 968. The Danevirke began as a defensive line to hold back the expansion of the Franks and Germans. In later years, it became a rallying point for Danes as they prepared to march south in "crusades" against the Slavs.

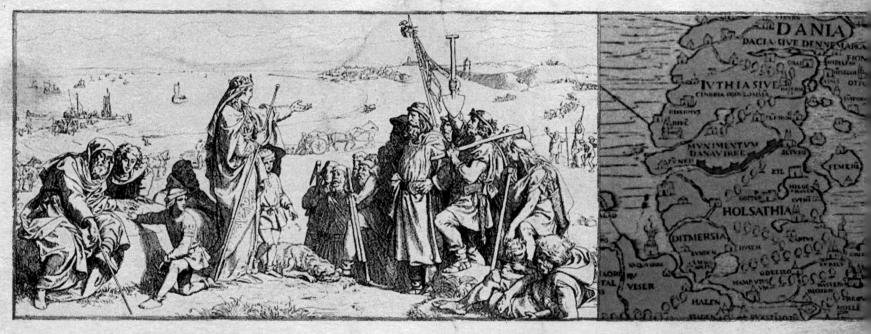

Left: Queen Thyra oversees the foundation of the Dane-work   Right: Illustration of the wall from Carta Marina

Fearful of Frankish and German expansion from the south, the Danish king Godfred extended the fortifications on the Danevirke. After he was murdered in 810, the region was plunged into a series of conflicts between his nephews and sons. Denmark was not properly unified for another century, until the long-lived Gorm the Old established a strong rule. His son, Harald Bluetooth, proclaimed himself the ruler of all Denmark, and also controversially converted to Christianity, moving his parents' remains from their pagan tombs and into the hallowed ground of a new church.

WHY DID THEY LEAVE SCANDINAVIA?

I t still is not certain what caused the mass exodus of young men to life on the sea that characterized the Viking Age in particular.

Ironically, prosperity might have been one of the causes, as warmer summers and milder winters allowed for good harvests and a general increase in the Scandinavian population. Better technology, particularly the arrival of the iron ax, permitted larger areas of forest to be cleared, encouraging further growth.

Daughters were often regarded as less worth preserving than sons, and many were left out in the wild to die. These factors might have combined to create a population of young men with no prospect of finding a wife or a place to live. All the good land was taken, and Scandinavian customs favored primogeniture—the inheritance of a man's estate by his eldest son. Younger sons might then hope to seek their fortunes abroad, as crew members on ships sailing off to trade with distant lands. If the trading turned bad, then they could always take what was not freely given.

21

From Viking to Farming...

In places where the Vikings encountered little or no resistance, such as Iceland or the Orkney Islands, they often ceased to qualify as Vikings at all, instead settling down as farmers or fishermen in their newfound land. However, even these peaceful settlements might only repeat the cycle a few generations later, as the good land ran out, and restless sons went in search of their own fortune, or fought over who got to inherit their father's wealth. In Denmark and Sweden, the locals could farm barley, oats, or peas. Here and in the rest of Scandinavia, they could also practice animal husbandry, raising cows, sheep, pigs, and goats, even on the limited pastures on the steep sides of fjords. One Viking Age village, Vorbasse in Jutland, has been fully excavated, and found to comprise a handful of homesteads sharing a common outer wall. Each raised a few cattle and a little corn. The village lacked any specialized industries, but in good times could generate surplus food that could be sold for metal tools, pottery, and even some luxuries from nearby towns such as Jelling or Hedeby.

...to Viking again

But if a village like Vorbasse faced lean times or found itself with too many mouths to feed, its young men might foray beyond their peaceful home to become Vikings once more.

Exiles and Refugees

Other men left Scandinavia for different reasons. Some were criminals evading the payment of a ransom for injuries done or murders committed. Others saw themselves as good folk who simply did not want to pay taxes or recognize the authority of the men who proclaimed themselves the rulers of Scandinavia. Many of the rich families of Iceland traced their origins back to people who fled Norway rather than submit to Harald Fairhair, the land's first king.

22

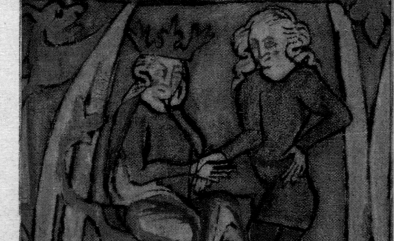

Fair Hair?

Harald Fairhair (c.880-c.930) supposedly got his nickname out of irony—he had sworn never to cut his hair until he succeeded in becoming the ruler of all Norway. It took many battles and negotiations before he was successful, by which point his hair fell past his waist and was a tangled mess.

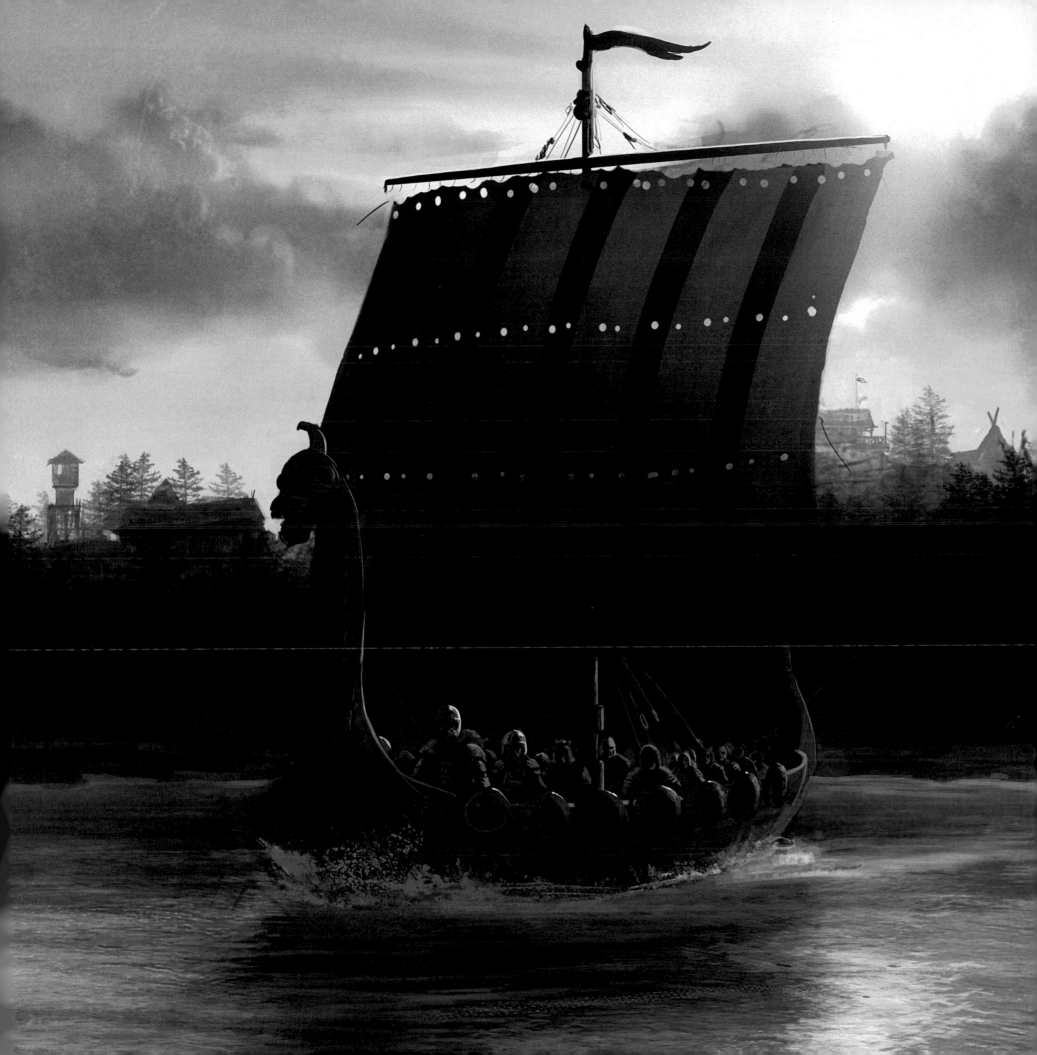

VIKING LEADERS

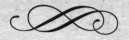

Viking society was loosely based on the organization of the place where the Vikings came from. In Scandinavia, isolated communities were organized into small districts, each led by an elected headman. What made someone a headman depended largely on strength—one might be the first settler in a region, the oldest wise man in a village, or an individual thought to have a special line of contact with the gods. In most cases, such authority still needed to be backed up with brute force. Headmen could call on their townsfolk in times of trouble.

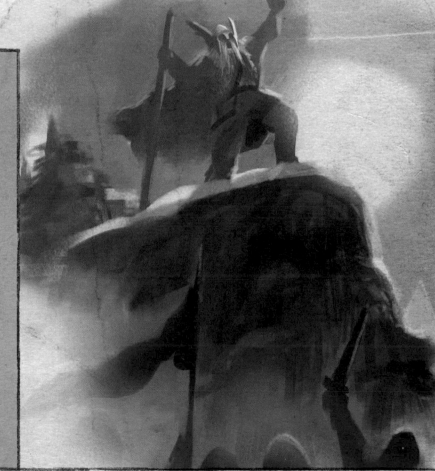

The Landthing

As villages grew in size and their reach stretched further, particular headmen enjoyed greater powers. They would eventually be called jarls (earls), who would meet an annual assembly (a Landthing) to debate the selection of a king, the declaration of war, or thorny legal cases.

Headmen might organize raids on other villages, sometimes in revenge for a perceived threat or insult, and other times simply for material gain. For Scandinavian villages on the seacoast, these raids could be carried out by ship. Raiders might even leave Scandinavia altogether and head across the Baltic or North Seas, to collect tribute in the form of amber, animal pelts, or other goods.

The Sea Kings

Simple village headmen, or jarls, were not Vikings. They might become Vikings during the summer raiding season, but they would return to their villages once the raiding was over. If a Scandinavian was temporarily banished, permanently exiled, or forced to flee from his home, he would become the ruler of nothing but his ship, with the loyalty of nothing but his crew. With nothing to lose and no home to call his own, he would go in search of land, wealth, or both on foreign shores. Such men were sometimes called "Sea Kings," in recognition of the fact that they had no domain but the waters on which they wandered.

A Viking war-band was run like a Scandinavian village stripped of everything but its ship. There was no room for women on a Viking ship—the Vikings would find wives where they landed, whether the women agreed or not. There was no room for cattle, pigs, or chickens—the Vikings would buy or steal them where they landed. There was room only for the Vikings, their weapons, and their stolen treasures.

Just as villages might band together into larger communities, Viking war-bands might gather into fleets. The strongest, most powerful leader would take overall charge, and the fleet would descend upon foreign lands. The robbers and raiders of the early Viking age hence transformed into great armies of pirates with nothing to lose.

25

great armies of pirates with nothing to lose

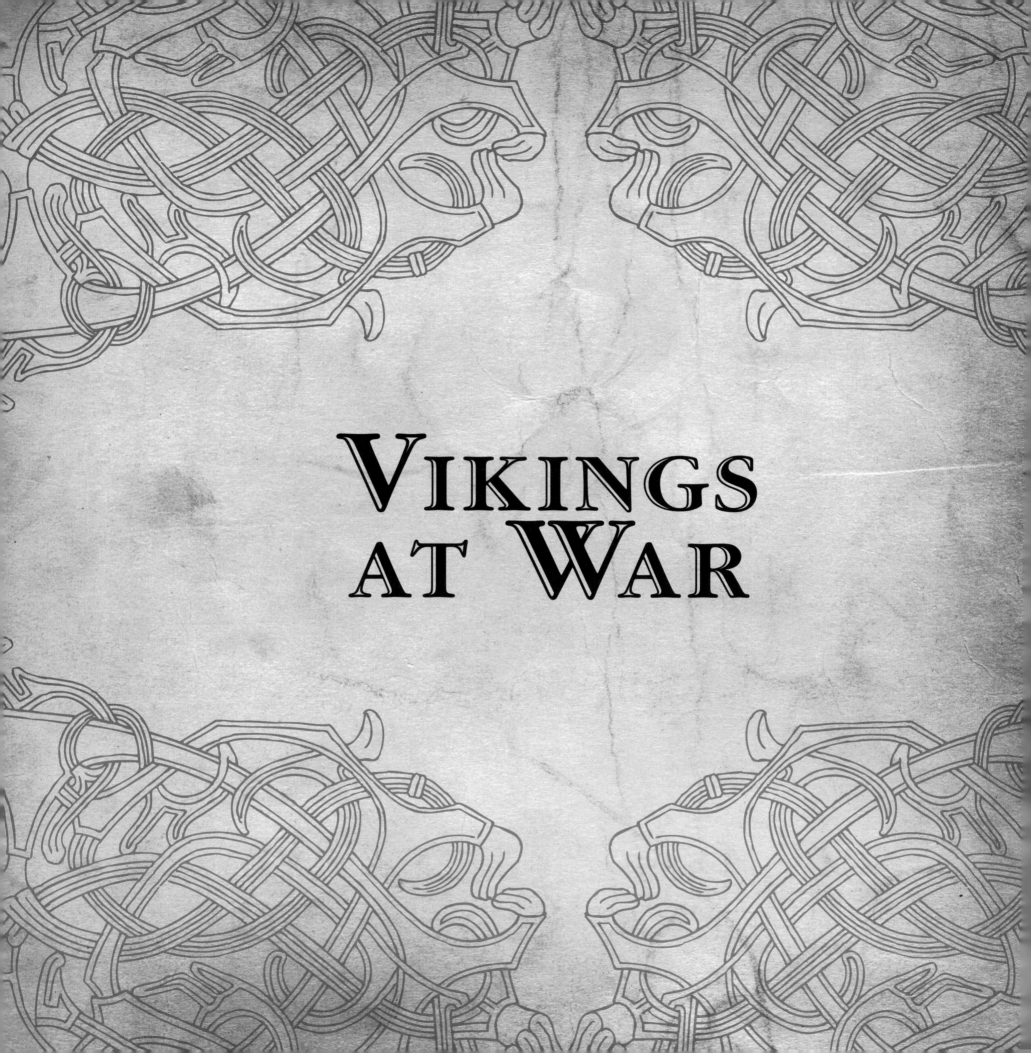

Vikings
at War

Viking Ships

The Vikings were excellent sailors. They were practiced in seamanship learned in the sheltered waters of the Baltic Sea and hardened by the terrifying experience of sailing out in the open seas of the Atlantic. Viking ships were lighter than their equivalents in other cultures. They had a low draft that permitted them to sail in shallow lakes and far up rivers, but were also kept light so that they could, if necessary, be lifted out of the water physically by the combined efforts of their crews. This was useful not only for dragging them up a beach for repairs, but also for "portage"—jumping from one lake or river to another. Portaging allowed Vikings to navigate far inland, and most notably to travel all the way across the European mainland from the Baltic to the Black Sea.

27

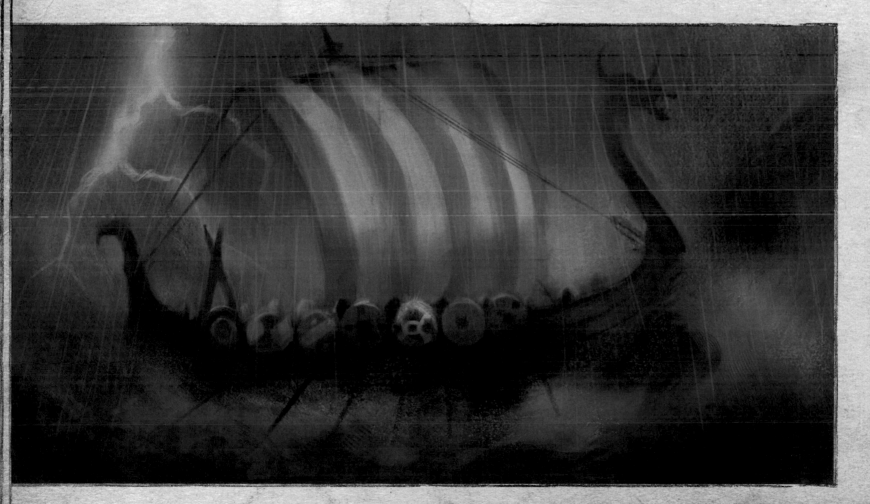

River Pirates

In the days before reliable roads and transport, rivers were the arteries of trade and commerce in Europe. We often think of the Vikings as solely sea-borne raiders, but it was their ability to travel on rivers that made them so dangerous to much of mainland Europe.

Ship Building

Scandinavian shipwrights used the clinker (also known as lapstrake) building technique, in which each plank overlapped the upper edge of the one below it. This gave the ships better flexibility in rough seas. Viking ships were usually double-ended, and could be "reversed" simply by changing the direction of rowing. The rudder or "steer-board" would be carried to the opposite end of the ship, and replaced, always at the right sight of the ship. Hence, the shipping terms "starboard" for right, and "port" for left (the side of the ship without the rudder, and therefore the side which would be moored closely against a jetty in a harbor). In later years, the dragon heads that sometimes formed fearsome adornments on the prows of Viking ships were made removable. As Christianity took hold, even some communities friendly to the Vikings refused to allow such frightening pagan objects into their harbors.

An unexpected bonus of clinker building is that the overlapping planks allow bubbles of air to force themselves along the hull of the ship as it rides through the waves. This cushions the ship and helps it slide more steadily through the water.

The abundance of sheltered and distant islands and fjords meant that power in Scandinavia relied upon mastery of the sea. This is why Viking leaders called themselves "sea kings." Our knowledge of their ships is based on references in sagas, occasional pictures, and a few vessels recovered from ship burials and undersea wrecks.

28

Woolen Sails

Surviving fragments of Viking sailcloth reveal that their sails were of wool, not linen. The Vikings wove their cloth from the tough waterproof wool of Scandinavian sheep, giving their ships strong and flexible sails.

Rigging

The rope that controlled a Viking sail was made of lime bast fiber or walrus hide. We do not know, however, precisely how Viking ships were rigged. There may have been dozens of ropes, manipulated by many crew members, to allow the sail to be turned swiftly to take optimal advantage of the wind.

The Skuldelev Ships

Late in the eleventh century, near the end of the Viking Age, the inhabitants of the Danish town of Skuldelev blocked a narrow channel on the approach to their homes. They did so by sinking five old ships—two cargo ships, a fishing boat, and two warships. Recovered by marine archaeologists in the 1960s, the Skuldelev ships have made a vital contribution to our understanding of how Viking vessels actually looked.

The wreck known as *Skuldelev 5* is a typical Viking warship. It sat low in the water, which made it difficult to spot in the distance if its sail was lowered. Fast and light, the ship sat only sat twenty inches deep in the water even when fully loaded. It could have easily raided far upstream on European rivers, or even been portaged across short distances by its crew. It would not have been much good in ocean waters, but was perfectly suited for coastal raiding. It was also a relatively small raider—its fellow wreck, *Skuldelev 2*, was almost twice the size, and could carry twice the crew.

29

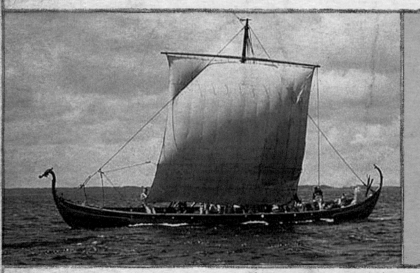

Skuldelev 5 Dimensions

Length: 57.41 ft
Width: 8.2 ft
Crew: 26 oarsmen
Speed*: 9 knots (sail), 5 knots (rowing)
(* Helge Ask, a modern replica of the Skuldelev 5 ship, achieved such speeds)

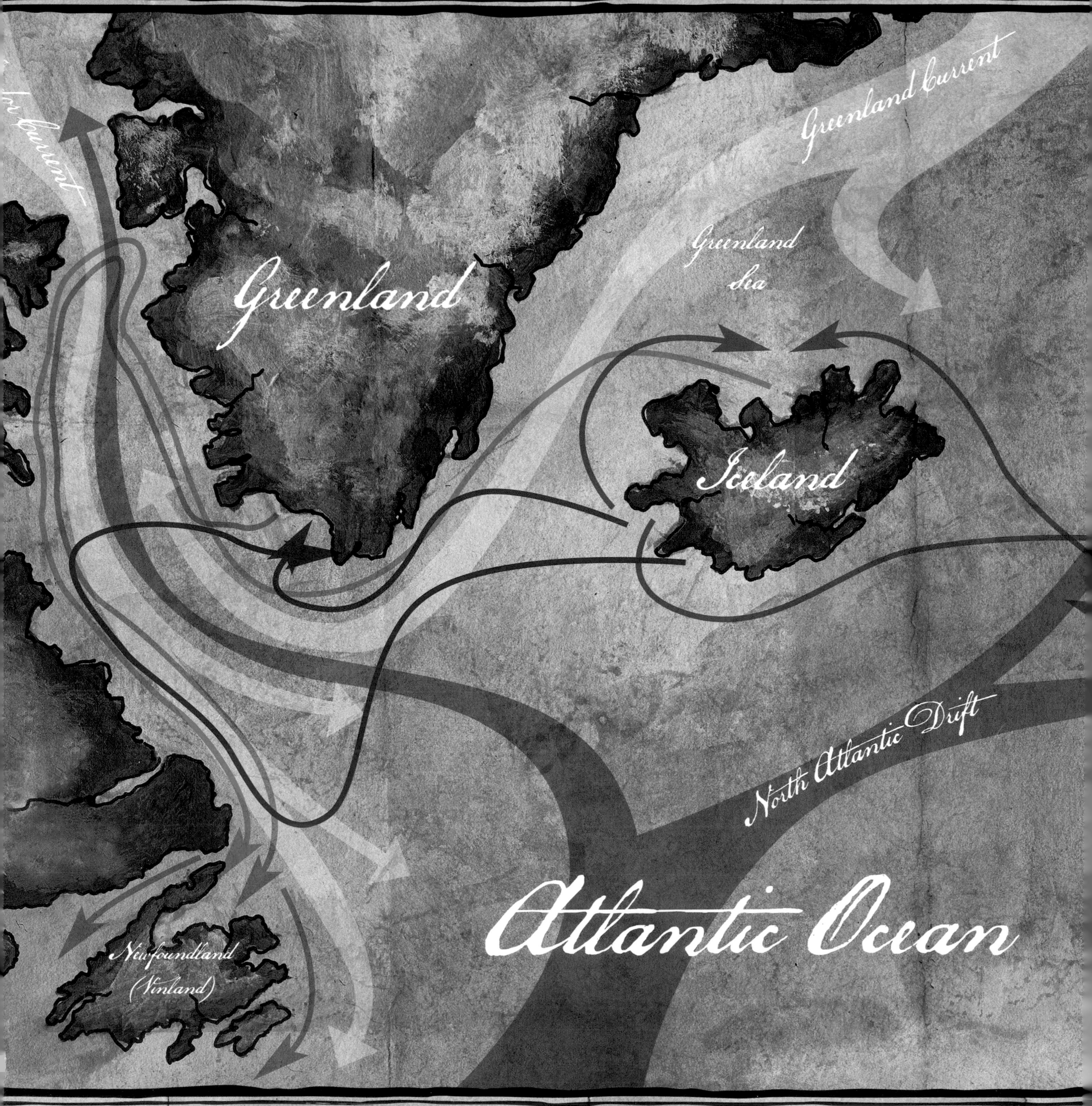
Greenland Current
Greenland
Greenland sea
Iceland
North Atlantic Drift
Atlantic Ocean
Newfoundland
(Vinland)

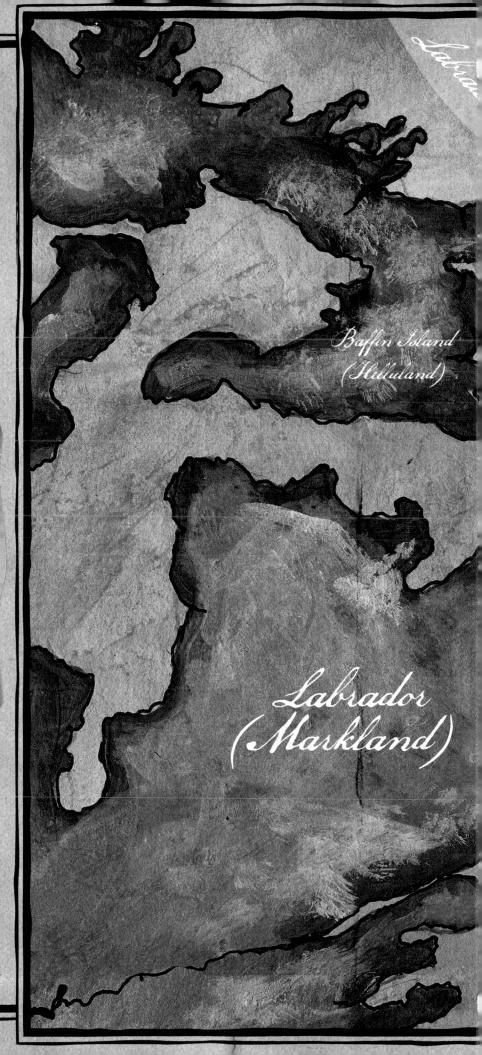

Leif Erikson

"…they saw land, and sailed to this land and came to an island, which lay to the north of the land, and went up there and looked about in fine weather and found that there was dew on the grass, and it happened to them, that they touched the dew with their hands and brought it to their mouths, and thought not to have known anything so sweet as this was."

– from *Saga of Erik the Red*

According to the Norse sagas, Leif Erikson and his crew sailed from Greenland and discovered America in A.D. 1000, nearly five hundred years before Columbus. Erikson named the newly-discovered land Vinland. In 1960 the remains of a Viking settlement were found in Newfoundland, Canada, by Norwegian archaeologists Helge Ingstad and Anne Stine Ingstad.

Baffin Island
(Helluland)

Labrador
(Markland)

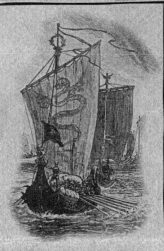

Voyage Legend

Early Voyages ➤

Erik the Red, 985 ➤

Bjarni Herjolfsson, 985-986 ➤

Leif Erikson, 1000 ➤

Thorfinn Karlsefni, c.1005 ➤

The Gokstad Ship

One of the most famous Viking vessels is the Gokstad ship, excavated in 1880 from a burial mound in southern Norway. Its owner, a chieftain who died around A.D. 900 had been buried with his ship completely intact, except for its mast, along with a number of sacrificial animals, including twelve horses, six dogs, and a peacock. It had sixteen pairs of oars, and thirty-two shields along its side—suggesting one Viking per oar. In 1893, shipwright and author Magnus Andersen sailed the *Viking*, a replica of the Gokstad ship, all the way from Scandinavia to North America in less than a month.

30

Gokstad Ship Dimensions

Length: 78.74 ft
Width: 16.4 ft
Crew: 32 oarsmen
Speed*: 12 knots (sail), 5 knots (rowing)
(* Viking, a modern replica of the Gokstad ship,
achieved such speeds)

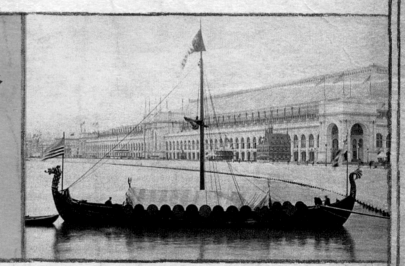

Navigation

We still do not know exactly how Vikings navigated—they probably used a combination of methods. In coastal waters, they could use prominent local onshore landmarks to determine their location. At sea, they had learned to use many fishermen's tricks, such as looking for clouds on the horizon (a sign of a nearby landmass), seabirds, or sudden calming of the water indicating a nearby island that could shield them from the worst of the weather. Sailors would also look for changes in the color of the water. The Viking explorer Raven-Floki got his name for the ravens he would periodically release on open sea. He located Iceland by following the flight path of the first raven not to return to his ship.

The Hillingar Effect

Sailors in the Arctic reported another means of finding land over the horizon: the "superior mirage," or hillingar effect. In certain conditions, mirages would create ghostly images of distant islands by bending light over the horizon.

The Solar Compass

Archaeologists in Greenland have found a wooden fragment that some believe to be a Viking solar compass. Sailors would have been able to navigate by watching the shadow of a central spindle. So far, the artifact is the only one of its kind. Surely if the Vikings used a solar compass, we would have found many more examples in wrecks and graves.

Out in the North Atlantic, some of the greatest Viking discoveries were made by accident. The Norwegian coast is a big target, and difficult to miss. Early Scandinavian sailors were thus encouraged to head west, secure in the knowledge that they could easily find their way home again once they turned back. Around 1000 A.D., Leif Erikson gained the nickname "the Lucky," after he successfully sailed from Greenland direct to Norway, without stopping halfway in Iceland. Reckless attempts to make the same journey in reverse probably led to the discovery by Leif Erikson of "Vinland" in North America.

31

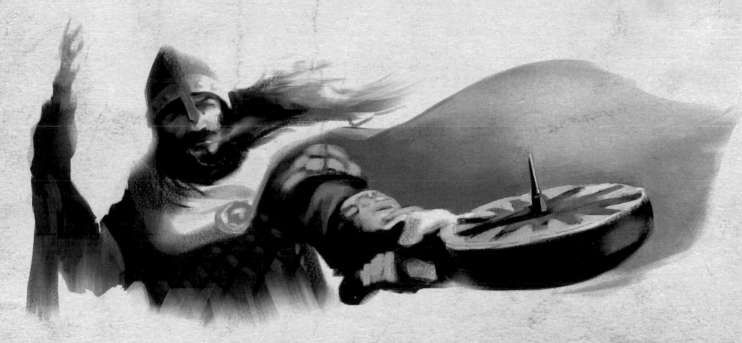

They afterward determined to establish themselves there for the winter, and they accordingly built a large house. There was no lack of salmon there either in the river or in the lake, and larger salmon than they had ever seen before. The country thereabouts seemed to be possessed of such good qualities that cattle would need no fodder there during the winters. There was no frost there in the winters, and the grass withered but little. The days and nights there were of more nearly equal length than in Greenland or Iceland. On the shortest day of winter, the sun was up between eykarstad and dagmalastad. When they had completed their house, Leif said to his companions, "I propose now to divide our company into two groups, and to set about an exploration of the country. One-half of our party shall remain at home at the house, while the other half shall investigate the land; and they must not go beyond a point from which they can return home the same evening, and are not to separate from each other." Thus they did for a time. Leif, himself, by turns joined the exploring party, or remained behind at the house. Leif was a large and powerful man, and of a most imposing bearing, a man of sagacity, and a very just man in all things.

It was discovered one evening that one of their company was missing; and this proved to be Tyrker, the German. Leif was sorely troubled by this, for Tyrker had lived with Leif and his father for a long time, and had been very devoted to Leif when he was a child. Leif severely reprimanded his companions, and prepared to go in search of him, taking twelve men with him. They had proceeded but a short distance from the house, when they were met by Tyrker, whom they received most cordially. Leif observed

at once that his foster-father was in lively spirits. Tyrker had a prominent forehead, restless eyes, small features, was diminutive in stature, and rather a sorry-looking individual withal, but was, nevertheless, a most capable handicraftsman. Leif addressed him, and asked, "wherefore art thou so belated, foster-father mine, and astray from the others?" In the beginning Tyrker spoke for some time in German, rolling his eyes and grinning, and they could not understand him; but after a time he addressed them in the Northern tongue: "I did not go much further than you, and yet I have something of novelty to relate. I have found vines and grapes." "Is this indeed true, foster-father?" said Leif. "Of a certainty it is true," quoth he, "for I was born where there is no lack of either grapes or vines." They slept the night through, and on the morrow Leif said to his shipmates, "we will now divide our labors, and each day will either gather grapes or cut vines and fell trees, so as to obtain a cargo of these for my ship." They acted upon this advice, and it is said that their after-boat was filled with grapes. A cargo sufficient for the ship was cut, and when the spring came they made their ship ready, and sailed away; and from its products Leif gave the land a name, and called it Vinland.

AN EXTRACT FROM THE SAGA OF THE GREENLANDERS DESCRIBING LEIF ERIKSON'S DISCOVERY AND EXPLORATION OF VINLAND (NORTH AMERICA).

There was now much talk about voyages of discovery. Leif, the son of Erik the Red, of Brattahlid, visited Biarni Heriulfsson and bought a ship from him, and collected a crew, until they formed altogether a company of thirty-five men. Leif invited his father, Erik, to become the leader of the expedition, but Erik declined, saying that he was then stricken in years, and adding that he was less able to endure the exposure of sea life than he had been. Leif replied that he would nevertheless be the one who would be most apt to bring good luck and Erik yielded to Leif's solicitation, and rode from home when they were ready to sail. When he was but a short distance from the ship, the horse which Erik was riding stumbled, and he was thrown from its back and wounded his foot, whereupon he exclaimed, "it is not designed for me to discover more lands than the one in which we are now living, nor can we now continue longer together." Erik returned home to Brattahlid, and Leif pursued his way to the ship with his companions, thirty-five men. One of the company was a German, named Tyrker. They put the ship in order; and, when they were ready, they sailed out to sea, and found first that land which Biarni and his shipmates found last. They sailed up to the land, and cast anchor, and launched a boat, and went ashore, and saw no grass there. Great ice mountains lay inland back from the sea, and it was as a land of flat rock all the way from the sea to the ice mountains; and the country seemed to them to be entirely devoid of good qualities. Then said Leif "it has not come to pass with us

in regard to this land as with Biarni, that we have not gone upon it. To this country I will now give a name, and call it Helluland." They returned to the ship, put out to sea, and found a second land. They sailed again to the land, and came to anchor, and launched the boat, and went ashore. This was a level wooded land; and there were broad stretches of white sand where they went, and the land was level by the sea. Then said Leif, "this land shall have a name after its nature; and we will call it Markland." They returned to the ship forthwith, and sailed away upon the main with north-east winds, and were out two days before they sighted land. They sailed toward this land, and came to an island which lay to the north of the land. There they went ashore and looked about them, the weather being fine, and they observed that there was dew upon the grass, and it so happened that they touched the dew with their hands, and touched their hands to their mouths, and it seemed to them that they had never before tasted anything so sweet as this. They went aboard their ship again and sailed into a certain sound, which lay between the island and a cape, which jutted out from the land on the north, and they stood in westering past the cape. At ebb-tide, there were broad reaches of shallow water there, and they ran their ship aground there, and it was a long distance from the ship to the ocean; yet were they so anxious to go ashore that they could not wait until the tide should rise under their ship, but hastened to the land, where a certain river flows out from a lake. As soon as the tide rose beneath their ship, however, they took the boat and rowed to the ship, which they conveyed up the river, and so into the lake, where they cast anchor and carried their hammocks ashore from the ship, and built themselves booths there.

The North Atlantic Voyages

Norwegian Sea

Norwegians

Swedes

North Sea

Baltic Sea

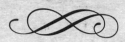 EARLY RAIDS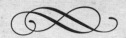

After the first appearances of criminals from the sea, local governments took various efforts to deal with the problem. In Anglo-Saxon Britain and the Empire of the Franks (France), rulers realized that Vikings would cause even greater havoc if they were permitted to sail upstream into unguarded regions, and subsequently established coastal defenses and fortified bridges to block the paths of potential raiders.

However, the Frankish Empire had troubles of its own after the death of its ruler Charlemagne in 815. This was particularly obvious in Frisia (the Netherlands), where local conflicts distracted the inhabitants. Emperor Louis the Pious granted a region of land on his northeast coast to Harald Klak, an exiled Danish king, in 826, in the hope that he could set Viking against Viking and thus preserve his realm inland. But such a plan seems to have backfired—new raiders simply went further east along the coast—and between the years 834 and 837, the major Frankish port of Dorestad was plundered four times.

32

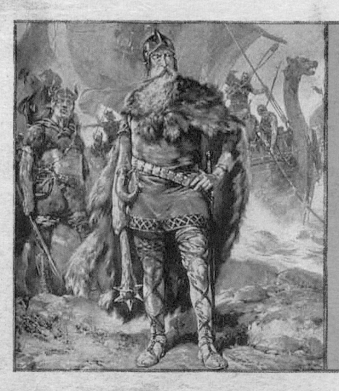

Viking against Viking?

Dorestad was eventually given to the Viking sea king, Roric, who had previously served the Franks as a mercenary. This suggests that the Franks had been using Viking against Viking in their conflicts for even longer than the history books indicate. Roric would prove a powerful ally in the battle against his countrymen.

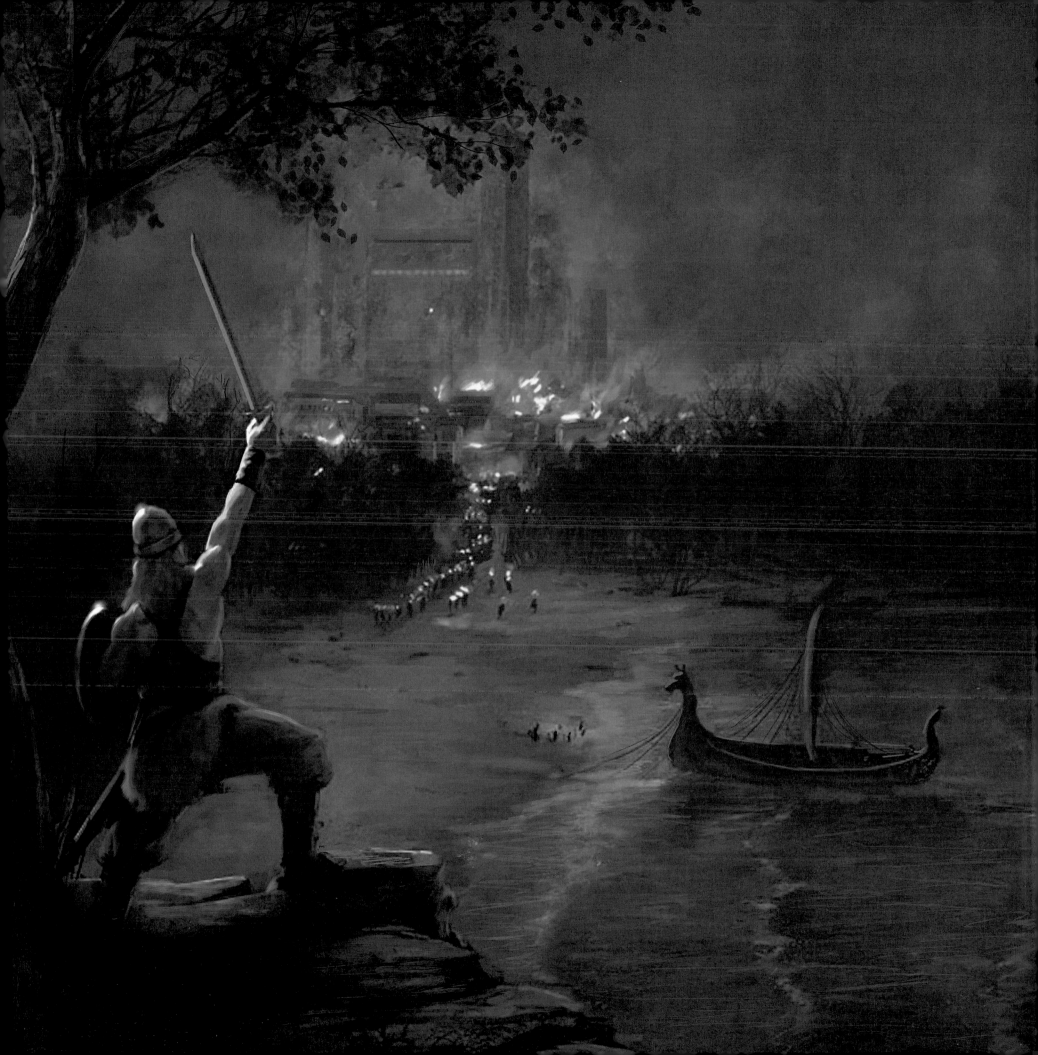

Raids became even more frequent after the death of Louis the Pious in 840. The Frankish Empire was divided between his three sons. The easternmost part, controlled by Louis the German, had very little coastline to raid. Lothar, who controlled middle part, largely kept Vikings out by extending the land grant to Harald Klak. It was the unlucky Charles the Bald who had the biggest problem—his kingdom had a coastline that occupied almost the entire north and west coasts of what is now France. Viking raiders sailed up the Seine River and sacked Paris in 845. Charles fought back by besieging a camp of Vikings in 858, but was forced to let them go when Lothar invaded.

34

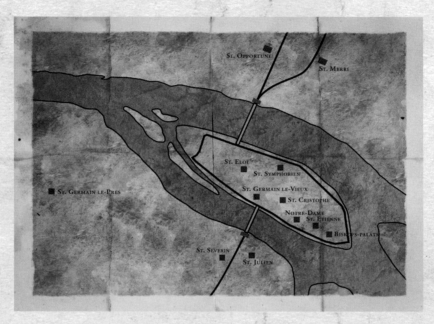

Above: A map of Paris in the ninth century

Danegeld

With the size of the Viking raiding parties now increased from mere handfuls of ships to veritable armies, Charles was obliged to pay invaders a bribe to leave him alone. The Vikings called it "tribute," although it was known locally as Danegeld—"Dane gold." Such bribes were paid to the Vikings on various occasions for the next two centuries. Even when Danegeld was not levied, sometimes it might as well have been—some English monarchs collected a heregeld, or army tax, designed to pay for military forces to prevent the need to bribe Vikings. The end result was, whether the Vikings attacked or not, local peasants ended up paying.

ARMS AND ARMOR

Viking battles did not begin as hand-to-hand melees, but with an exchange of thrown missiles. The Vikings were keen archers, and target shooting was one of their most popular games. Some European races (such as the Ancient Greeks) regarded the bow a coward's weapon, but there are many proud references in Viking stories of warriors fighting with arrows instead of swords.

Sticks and Stones

Not all references in Viking sagas are to be believed. Some mention crossbows, which were not in widespread use at the time of the Viking era, although they were well known a century later when many Viking stories were first written down. Some also describe Vikings using slings, but this is unlikely. These would have been difficult weapons to use in close combat, and are instead likely to be leftovers from later Christian writers' readings of the Bible—particularly the story of David and Goliath. However, Vikings defending a building such as a fortress might use their bare hands to drop stones on attackers.

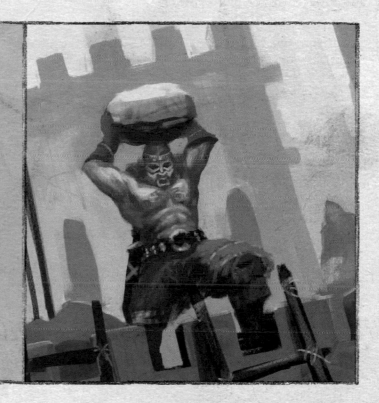

35

Vikings used spears in close combat, but also as throwing weapons. Viking throwing spears were often used after the removal of the pin that held the head onto the shaft. This would effectively make the spear fall apart if picked up by the other side, rendering it useless to the enemy after it had been thrown once.

Swords of Legend

Many Vikings used axs or spears for fighting, since these required less metal and were cheaper to produce. But the pinnacle of Viking weaponry was the sword—over 2,000 have been found in Scandinavian graves, although many of them are not of Scandinavian origin. Frankish and English swordsmiths were the most highly prized, leading to unsuccessful attempts by the Vikings' enemies to prevent merchants selling imported weapons in Scandinavia. Many swords were passed on as family heirlooms, and were often used for generations. According to legend, the finest sword ever seen was an English creation, a gift from King Athelstan to his Christian foster-son King Hakon of Norway (c.920-960). It was called Quernbiter, in honor of its supposed ability to slice through a millstone.

36

Cursed Blades?

Many Viking swords were stolen—either lifted from corpses after a battle or pillaged from tombs of other warriors. Viking sagas also mention occasions when the value of a sword led to fights and quarrels. The sword Legbiter, stolen from an Icelander by his fleeing wife, was supposedly cursed to bring the death of every man who touched it. The sword Greyside, probably of Irish origin, led to a quarrel between its owner Kol and the man who had borrowed it. The fight ended with the sword broken and both men dead.

Back Up

Few Vikings went anywhere without a small knife, which they used for eating, as a shipboard tool, or for last-ditch protection. Called a sax, it was not part of the military arsenal, but could be just as lethal.

Strength and Shield

The main form of protection for a Viking was his shield. Usually, these were round, roughly three feet in diameter, made of wood, sometimes coated with leather, and with a metal "boss" in the center over the place where the Viking's hand would be. The shield was not merely for protection, but could be used in the heat of battle as a makeshift club, as Vikings pushed and shoved against their enemies. When sailing, the shields could be hung on the sides of the ship for extra protection, although this was usually done only for show, when a ship was in a harbor, or when the crew expected they would soon be rowing into battle. Toward the end of the Viking Age, Vikings also adopted the longer kite-shaped shields of the Norman model. These afforded better protection to the otherwise exposed legs of horsemen, and could also be driven into the ground to make temporary barriers when a Viking required that both his hands be free. Such shields, however, came so late in the Viking Age that the people who used them were barely Vikings at all.

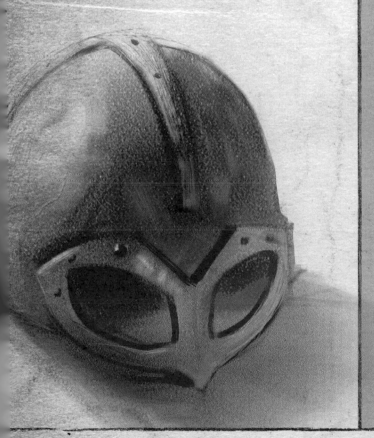

Horn-Free

There is remarkably little evidence surviving of the use of helmets for head protection in the early Viking Age—it is likely that, if they covered their heads at all, the Vikings and their foes more often used leather protectors. After the eleventh century, when "Vikings" were more likely to be fighting in invading armies or as mercenary soldiers, they often adopted the headgear of their enemies or employers. The sole surviving example of a helmet made by Vikings for Vikings is the Germundbu helmet from around A.D. 880, a relatively basic steel cap with a guard over the wearer's eyes. They may have often been more decorative than practical. There is no evidence of the use of horned helmets, which were impractical and unbalanced affectations that would have given the attacked something to grab onto. These appear to have been a development of later fictions—particularly artists of the nineteenth century and modern Hollywood filmmakers.

37

Armor

Heavy armor was a liability in marine combat, likely to weigh down a warrior and drown him if he slipped and fell. On land, however, most Vikings protected themselves with tough leather clothes. The richer or more powerful Vikings, particularly in the later Viking Age, wore tunics of chain mail. These suits of thousands of tiny links could prevent most cuts, although sometimes the blunt force of a blow was enough to injure an opponent, whether he was wearing armor or not. King Harald the Ruthless of Norway had a coat of mail that covered so much of him, from a distance it looked like a dress, causing his men to give it (or possibly him) the nickname "Emma." Archaeological evidence from many battlefields suggests that a soldier's legs were a prime target in battle, as mail protected most other parts of his body. Viking archers or swordsmen aimed for the head or legs, and hoped to finish off an opponent once he was down. Harald the Ruthless met his end in just such a fashion, stabbed from below, under his infamous mail "skirt."

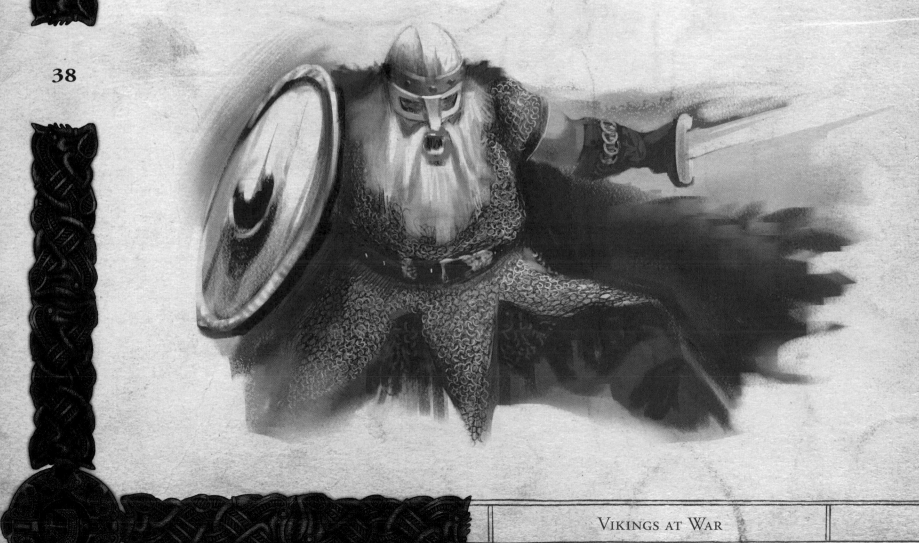

❧ VIKINGS ON TOUR ❧

With most parts of the north coast of France either occupied by other Vikings, well defended by the Franks, or simply already plundered, Viking raiders sailed even further to the west. As ever, their true shock tactics were reflected in their lack of respect toward Christian institutions. Nantes was attacked during the festival of St. John the Baptist in 843, by a Viking fleet operating in secret collusion with the corrupt local lord, Count Lambert. The venture got out of hand when the Vikings stormed the cathedral, killing the local bishop and many priests and civilians who had hoped to take refuge in the church.

Reading between the lines of surviving accounts, the multiple Viking raids reported during the 840s were the work of just two powerful groups of Viking ships—one on the Seine River that led to Paris, and another on the Loire River that reached deep into mainland France. The Loire group, however, was eventually bought off with Danegeld, and sailed even further along the coast, plundering first Aquitaine, and then the northern coast of Spain, where they were beaten back by fierce local resistance.

They enjoyed better luck in Lisbon, where they were left to sack the city without much resistance, and conducted similar raids on ports further to the south at the entry to the Mediterranean. This took them out of the notice of Christendom, since southern Spain was a Muslim territory at the time. However, it was in the Muslim world that they suffered their first major defeat, when they attempted to repeat tactics that had served them well in Northern Europe. The Viking raiders sailed up the Guadalquivir River in 844, captured the city of Seville, and then made the fatal mistake of leaving their ships to raid the area nearby. There, a Muslim army dealt them a crushing defeat, reporting 1,000 enemies dead, 400 prisoners, and thirty ships destroyed. A paltry handful of survivors fled for their lives with little more than the clothes on their backs, and they eventually made it back to the Loire.

Into the Mediterranean

The disaster at Seville kept Vikings out of the Muslim world until 859, when leaders Hastein and Bjorn Ironside returned in force, with a fleet of sixty-two ships. They encountered coastal resistance much like their predecessors, but dealt with it in typical Viking style by sailing ever onward in search of easier pickings. This brought them through the Straits of Gibraltar into the Mediterranean, where they took Muslim towns in North Africa by surprise, before falling upon the Mediterranean coast of Spain. However, resistance was still relatively strong, and the Vikings soon left the Muslims behind, arriving, much to the surprise of the Franks, on the Mediterranean coast of France.

Hacksilver

When Vikings plundered churches and monasteries, they were often interested solely in the precious metals, not in the artifacts themselves. Accordingly, Vikings often destroyed priceless Christian relics to get at the gold, silver, or gems. Precious metals would be either melted down or smashed to be divided among a Viking war band. Such fragments of ruined treasure are known as hacksilver, and were often used as a form of currency among Vikings, in lieu of real coins.

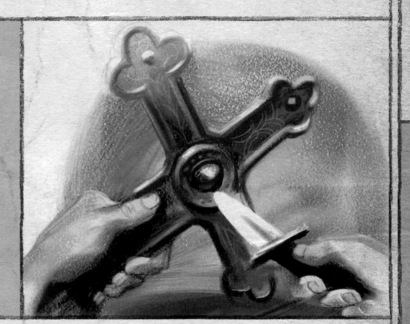

40

They spent the winter of 859-860 on an island near the mouth of the Rhône River, before sailing upriver in the spring to sack Valence. Resistance, however, was still strong, prompting the Vikings to sail on to the relatively lowly town of Luna in north Italy.

Hastein and Bjorn left Italy with their men, but their destination is unknown. It is thought that they may have continued raiding in the eastern Mediterranean or North Africa, but their whereabouts for the rest of 860 are unclear. By 861, they were back off the coast of Spain, where their luck ran out. A Muslim fleet delivered a second crushing blow, leaving barely a third of the original fleet to limp home to the Loire, stopping only to plunder Pamplona.

The Viking grand tour of the Mediterranean was never repeated. Despite their reputation for long voyages, when it came to raiding the Vikings preferred to have a firm base from which they could mount a series of short attacks. Where such a base was possible, the Vikings often became permanent residents. But the raiders in Spain and beyond never got a permanent foothold, and hence had little desire to return. As for Rome, their apparent target, they somehow missed it, and the city remained safe from them.

THE EMPIRE STRIKES BACK

Bjorn Ironside and Hastein may have been tempted to seek new victims owing to developments in the Frankish Empire. After years of internal strife, the Frankish King Charles the Bald finally settled his differences with his brothers, and was ready to take on his unwelcome Scandinavian guests.

The Fake Funeral

Believing they had reached Rome, a city renowned for its treasures but also for its military prowess, Hastein gained entry to Luna by a new ruse. His men carried him into the city in a coffin, claiming that he had died and sought Christian burial to atone for his Viking sins. Instead, Hastein was very much alive, and leaped from his coffin during his own funeral, stabbing the officiating bishop. The Vikings learned later that they were not in Rome after all—leading them to kill in anger all the men in the city whom they had not already murdered.

41

Frankish King Charles the Bald finally settled his differences with his brothers

Double Agents

In 860, Charles the Bald paid a Viking named Weland 5000 lbs. of silver to fight off any of his countrymen that might sail up the Seine. The plan seemed to work when Weland managed to trap an entire raiding party on the Isle of Oissel. However, the Vikings offered him 6000 lbs. of silver as a bribe, and he allowed them to escape. The incident demonstrated a perennial problem with using Vikings to fight Vikings—they had no loyalty to anything except money.

Charles initiated a series of programs across his section of the Frankish Empire, designed to hold the Vikings back. He gave up on the lower parts of the rivers, where the Vikings already had strongholds. But further upstream, old towns had their ruined Roman-era walls restored. Fortified bridges were built on the Seine and the Loire.

42

Pont de l'Arche

The highlight of Charles's program was the bridge at Pont de l'Arche, near Pitres, on the Seine River. Two fortified areas on either side of the river were linked by an equally strong bridge, allowing occupants a firm position from which to fight any Vikings that came upstream. The construction of the bridge was delayed by Viking attacks, but once completed around 870, it worked well. A single major Viking attack was fought off in 876, giving the upper Seine an entire decade free of the Vikings. The bridge, however, was destroyed in a later Viking attack.

Feudal Lords

Despite Charles's efforts to protect his subjects, the best solution to the Viking problem lay in localized defenses. Local leaders who were able to organize anti-Viking militia were able to react with a speed that matched the Vikings' own raids. The strengthening of defenses, and the readiness of local militia, helped deter the Vikings, as did the news that richer, easier pickings awaited somewhere else: England.

THE GREAT HEATHEN HOST

England in the late ninth century was not yet a single unified country, but instead was a patchwork of smaller kingdoms. Although it was left alone for some periods, it came to be regarded as a prime target by the Vikings, not merely for plunder, but also for settlement, either by seizure from its previous owners, or simply by finding unsettled areas—much of what the locals considered to be poor land was actually rather high quality by Scandinavian standards.

The English had no idea of the Vikings' intentions or of their origins. One reason for the apparent increase in attacks came from the number of Viking bases outside Scandinavia. The *Anglo-Saxon Chronicle* called all the attackers "Danes," but while some had come directly from Denmark and Norway, others sailed from Ireland, Scotland, and France, where earlier plunders had exhausted the local supply.

The first clue of increased Viking numbers came in 850, when a vast force of 350 ships wintered on the Isle of Thanet in the southeastern corner of the British Isles. The Vikings went on the offensive in 851, attacking both Canterbury and London, before running into superior forces somewhere up the River Thames.

43

[In 866] came a large heathen army into England, and fixed their winter-quarters in East-Anglia, where they were soon horsed; and the inhabitants made peace with them.
—Anglo-Saxon Chronicle

the English had no idea of the Vikings' intentions or their origins

More Vikings were back in 865, but this time they left their ships behind. They landed in East Anglia and made for Thetford, where, as had happened so often in the past, local people bought them off. This time, they were bribed not with money, but with horses, all the better to ensure they left the kingdom with great speed. The Viking raiders, now an even more fearsome mounted cavalry, rode to the northern kingdom of Northumbria, then in the middle of a civil war.

This time the Vikings had a purpose. They were led by three brothers, Halfdan, Ubbe, and Ivar the Boneless, who claimed to be the sons of one Ragnar Lodbrok, a Viking who had been killed on the order of the King Aella of Northumbria, who had him thrown into a pit of snakes. Thus, they were not merely raiders, but avengers of their murdered father.

Fighting in Northumbria went on for several years, at the end of which the Vikings were victorious and York (Jorvik) became the capital of a new Viking kingdom. The rival kings of old Northumbria united against the new foe, but were both killed.

44

The Blood Eagle

Later Viking stories held that the Vikings saved a special fate for Aella, the killer of Ragnar. He was tied down and subjected to the "blood eagle" sacrifice, in which his ribs were smashed away from his spine and his lungs pulled out and spread across his back like wings. However, no contemporary accounts actually describe this event; they merely report that Aella "died." It is possible that "blood eagle" was simply a kenning (a poetic reference), and was intended to mean that Aella's dead body was left out for the ravens.

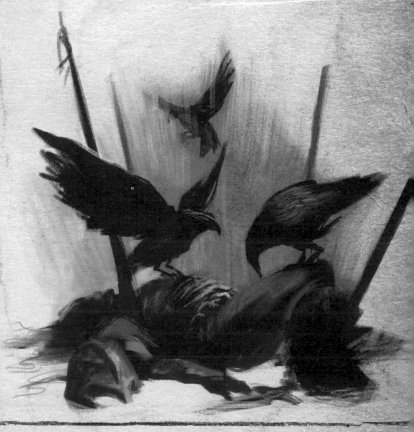

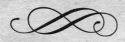

~~ Alfred the Great ~~

The Great Heathen Host now had a strong base in Northumbria from which to plunder the rest of the British Isles. Halfdan led his men north in 874, while the vast body of the Great Heathen Host headed south, plundering much of Mercia and East Anglia in the ensuing decade. The Viking attacks would destroy the old kingdoms, plunging the entire island into chaos. But it was the resistance against them, mounted from the southernmost kingdom of Wessex, which would halt them in their tracks and create the kingdom of England as a by-product.

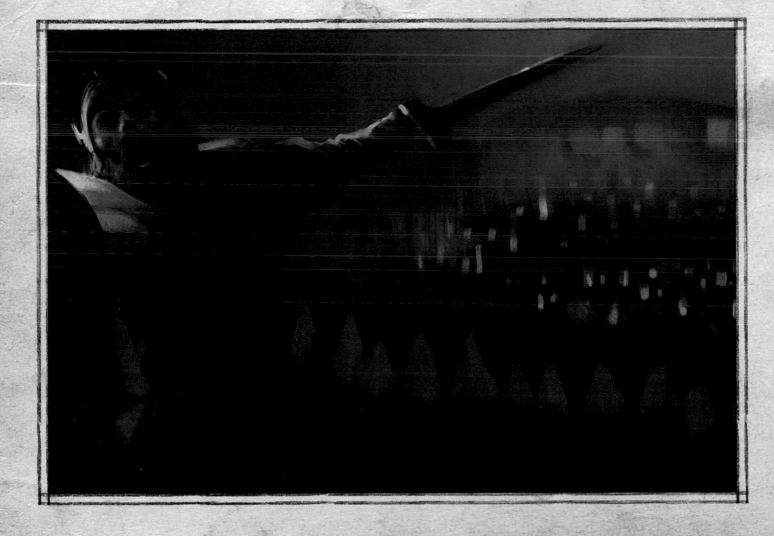

By 874, a group of Vikings led by one Guthrum had crossed over into Wessex, where they left a trail of destruction. The young new local king, Alfred, led a series of ill-fated operations against them, but often his actions amounted to little more than nipping at their heels as they plundered town after town. On the south coast of England at Wareham, Alfred finally managed to make a treaty with Guthrum, who swore on a ring of Thor that he would leave. Guthrum broke his oath, however, and headed even further south. Bottled in at Exeter, he seems to have planned to disappear ahead of his pursuers, but was foiled when storms sank the 120-ship rescue fleet that was supposed to extract him.

Eventually, a bribe worked where oaths would not, and Guthrum's army temporarily quit Wessex to plunder territory to its north. But by 878, the number of potential targets was decreasing. Half of Mercia was now settled by Vikings, and Guthrum turned his attentions once more to Wessex. He did so in a surprise attack, falling upon his enemies in the midst of their Christmas celebrations—Vikings were used to fighting in the cold; what's more, they knew that the English would not be expecting an attack in midwinter.

46

On the Run

On the run after the defeat, Alfred supposedly hid in the marshes of Athelney. Not realizing the identity of her royal guest, a swineherd's wife yelled at him for allowing her cakes to burn when he was supposed to be watching the fire. Later, Alfred shared a fish with a stranger, who turned out to be Saint Cuthbert in disguise, and who promised to give him supernatural aid against the Vikings. According to another legend, Alfred turned the tables on the Vikings by disguising himself as a minstrel or juggler and performing in their camp. While he did so, he learned of their plans. However, none of these stories were written down until several centuries after the events they describe.

Led by Alfred, the English fought the Viking invaders to a standstill at the Battle of Edington. Afterward, Alfred secured a guarantee from the Viking leader Guthrum: The Vikings could keep the lands that they had already taken in the east of England, but they had to convert to Christianity. Guthrum accepted this strange request, and was baptized as Alfred's new godson.

The Vikings and the English now shared the land of the British Isles by way of an uneasy truce. The Vikings kept their ways and laws in their own territory, although as time passed, some began to take their Christian conversion more seriously.

Alfred's truce with Guthrum was also a cunning variation on the same settlement agreements that the Franks had made along the coast of northern France. The next time Vikings attacked the east coast of England, they would have to fight other Vikings—or rather former Vikings who now had a vested interest in fighting to protect their hard-won lands.

47

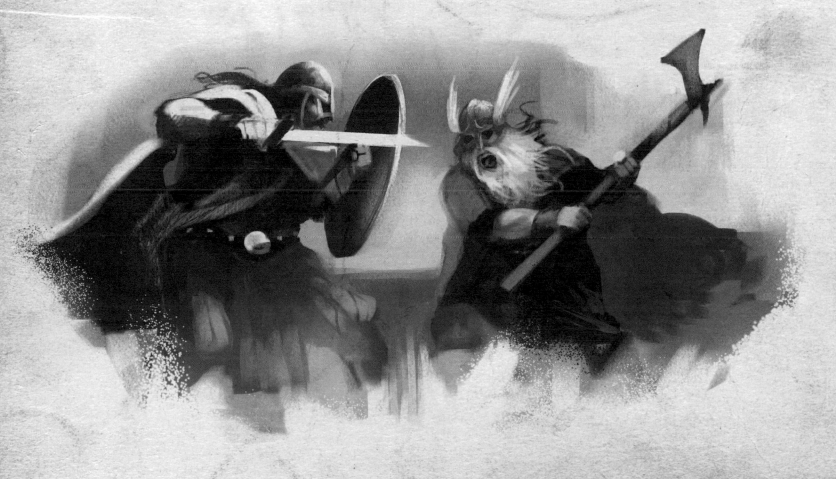

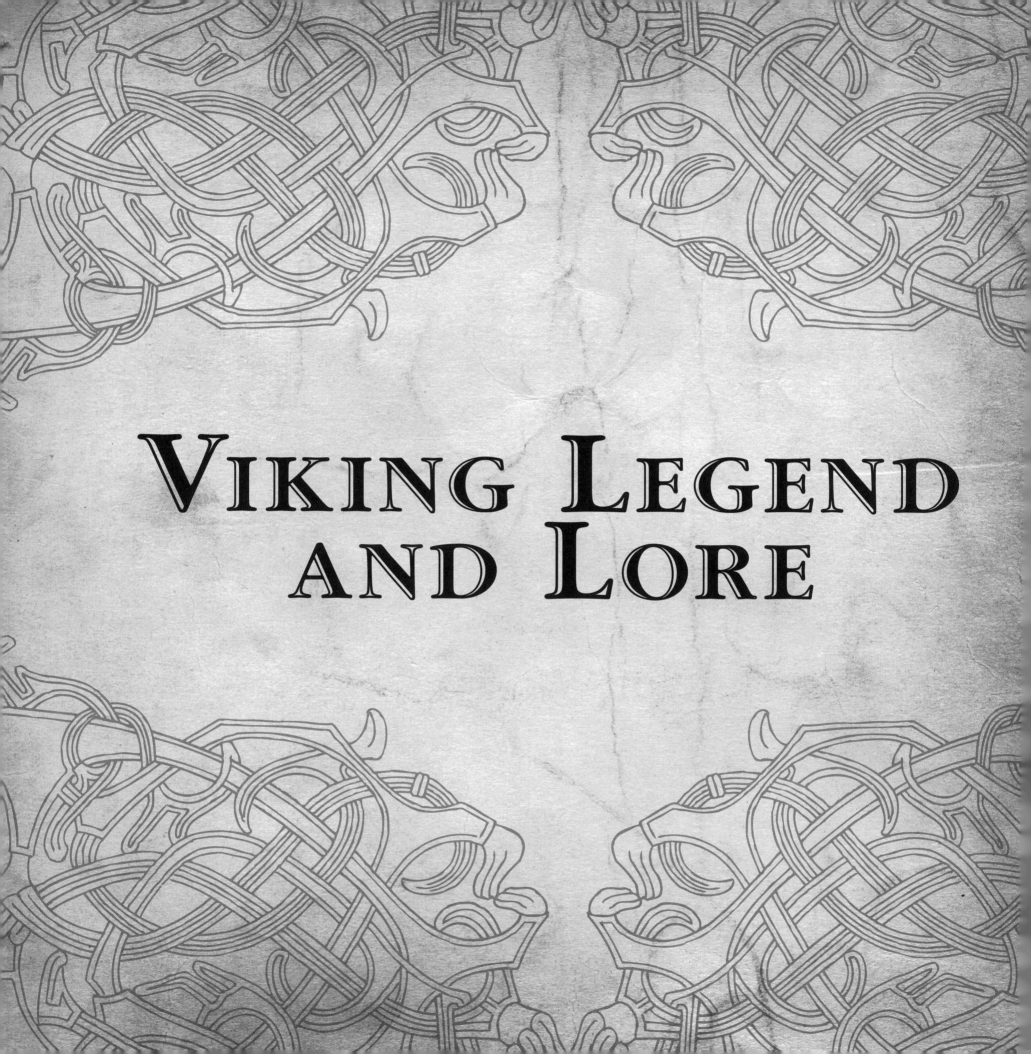

VIKING LEGEND
AND LORE

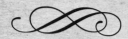
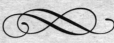

WORDS OF THE VIKINGS

The Vikings placed great value on words. They took praise very seriously, and repaid insults with deadly force. Like many in pagan Europe, they regarded writing as a magical means of communication, and associated their letter-carvings, or runes, with the power of the gods.

The Runic Alphabet

Runes were used throughout pagan Europe, but the Vikings used a version called the Younger Futhark—an adaptation of an earlier script, the Older Futhark (see below), which takes its name from the first six runes: ᚠ (f) ᚢ (u) ᚦ (th) ᚨ (a) ᚱ (r) ᚲ (k). Each rune made a sound, but also had a hidden meaning if used on its own.

ᚠ	cattle wealth	ᛇ	yew (wood)
ᚢ	water	ᛈ	pear
ᚦ	giant, monster	ᛉ	elk
ᚨ	god	ᛋ	sun
ᚱ	riding, chariot	ᛏ	Tiwaz (the god Tyr)
ᚲ	ulcer, illness	ᛒ	birch
ᚷ	gift	ᛖ	horse
ᚹ	joy	ᛗ	man
ᚺ	hail	ᛚ	lake
ᚾ	need	ᛜ	Ingwaz (the god Frey)
ᛁ	ice	ᛞ	day
ᛃ	year	ᛟ	estate

49

Viking runic inscriptions have been found carved as graffiti, on wooden labels used by merchants, and on weapons and gravestones. Their angular shape makes it easier to carve them into stone.

The Legend of the Runes

According to Norse legend it was Odin that gained knowledge of the runes through self-sacrifice. The Hávamál (one of the poems in the *Poetic Edda*) describes Odin's discovery:

"I know that I hung on a windy tree
nights all nine,
wounded with a spear and given to Odin,
myself to myself,
on that tree of which no man knows from where its roots run
No bread did they give me nor a drink from a horn,
downwards I peered,
I took up the runes,
screaming I took them,
then I fell back from there"

Some scholars believe that Viking-age shamans or followers of Odin used runes for divination or to demonstrate other-worldly powers.

Runology

People who study Runic alphabets and inscriptions are called runologists. The first runologist was a Swedish scholar, and adviser to the Swedish King, named Johannes Bureus (1568-1652). Modern runologists study the more than 6,000 runic inscriptions that exist today, first transcribing the inscription into Old Norse (the language used during the Viking Age) and then translating into English. The work of Runologists has added greatly to our understanding of the Vikings and their history.

downwards I peered, I took up the runes

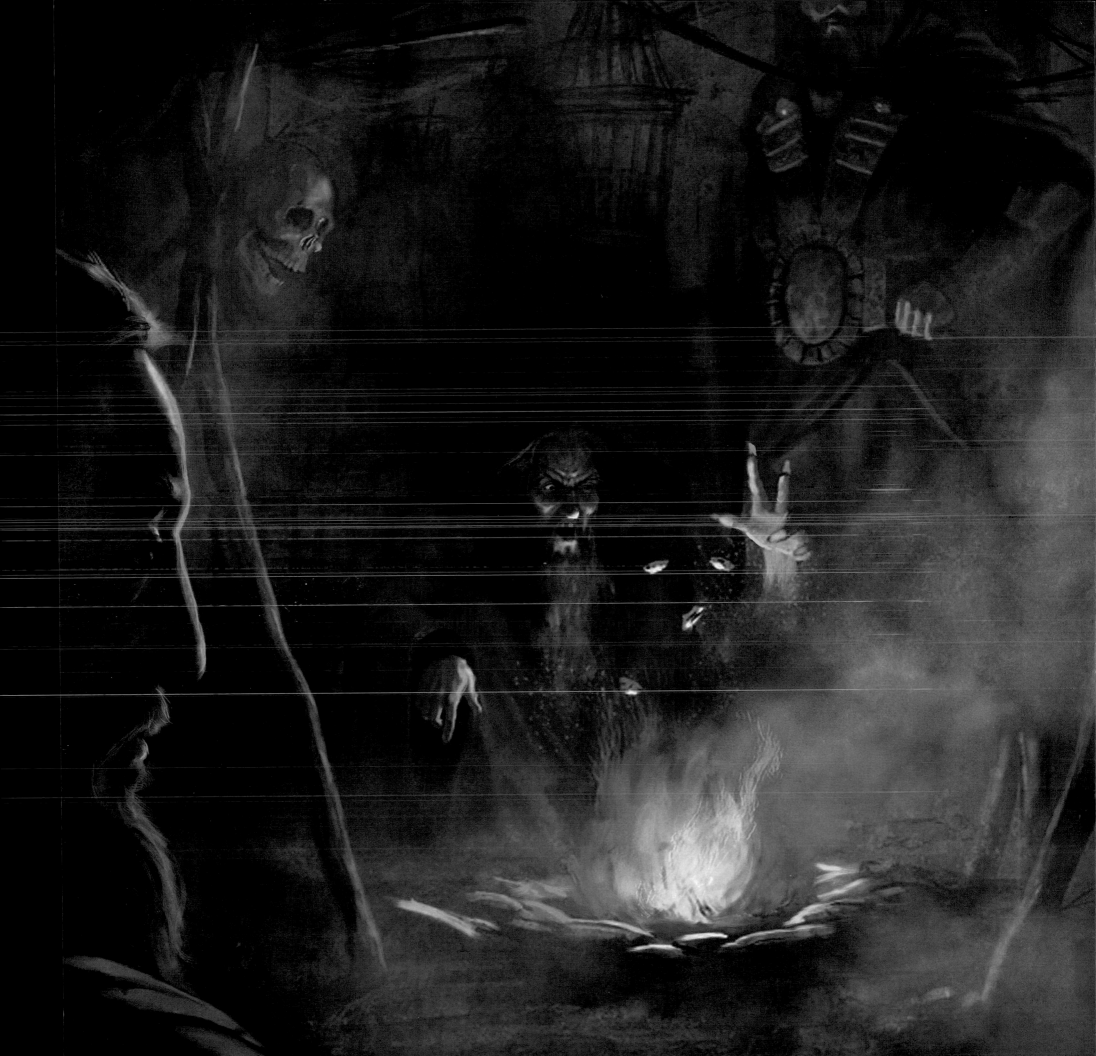

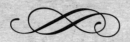 VIKING SONGS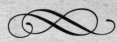

Viking entertainers were called skalds (poets). They were called upon to sing songs and tell tales of the deeds of the war band, and were prized for their ability to remember a warrior's greatest moments. Skalds would sometimes exaggerate, but rarely boasted too much of a Viking's achievements, or else risked a hail of cups, bones, and other missiles from an angry crowd. Skalds memorized their songs and rarely wrote them down, making it virtually impossible to know much about them today. Most songs recorded in Viking sagas were only written down many decades after the time the song was first performed, and the words may have been altered over time.

52

Kennings

Because of the kennings (poetic references), Viking texts are sometimes hard to understand. Skalds prided themselves on using obscure poetic references to everyday things, particularly when referring to battles, which would otherwise devolve into a dreary catalogue of stabbings and deaths. A "sword dance" could refer to a battle, a "blood worm" could be a sword, and a "necklace sleigh" might be a woman (named for the jewelery she wore). Here are some other examples:

KENNING	EXPLANATION	DEFINITION
Mountain of hawks	place where hawks perched	arm/hand
Drawer of swords	person who wields weapons	warrior
Ruiner of shields	person who smashes enemies	warrior
Wolf feeder	person who leaves dead meat	warrior
Bees of wounds	things that sting	arrows
Swan of blood	a bird found on battlefields	raven
Sea steed	something that travels on the sea	ship
Sea steed's path	where a ship travels	the sea
Bone rain	liquid that falls from bones	blood

Some of the most complicated Viking kennings virtually defy understanding:

"Glorious gleam-possessors of the dark, storm skilled horse of the bed of the swan"

Persons with shining objects who are on the vehicle that floats on water (warriors)

"Often night-traveling horse of wife of Ygg or river bone"

The beast like that ridden by the legendary wife of Ygg (a wolf)

Most of the Viking verse that has survived seems to celebrate battle or the worship of particular gods. Much extant Viking verse was recorded in Iceland, where, sadly, love poems were illegal, since locals feared they could be used to conceal spells. Thus, we have little idea how a skald might have tried to impress girls.

53

GODS AND LEGENDS OF THE VIKINGS

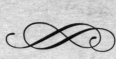 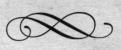

The Vikings were a mystery to their victims, savage enemies who paid no heed to Christian ways. But the Vikings had gods of their own, a series of legends and lore about ancient deities whom they hoped would protect them from harm and bless them in battle.

Viking religion was a mix of ancestor worship and superstition. They believed in good and evil spirits, in curses and blessings, and in supernatural creatures who would give them magical powers in return for sacrifices and great deeds.

We will never know the entire truth about the gods and myths of Scandinavia. The Vikings ignored the stories and characters that were of no interest to them, leaving us with scant records of gods of women, farmers and fishermen. But around their campfires and ship's masts, the Vikings would happily tell and re-tell stories of the gods of war and battle.

54

The Father of Viking Myth

Much of what we know today of Viking mythology comes to us through a single major source—the medieval writer Snorri Sturluson. Snorri was born too late to have seen the Viking Age, living from 1179-1241. He came from one of the most prominent families in medieval Iceland, and served three terms as the Lawspeaker—the highest political office on the island at the time. Snorri was a Christian, but he had a great interest in the beliefs of his ancestors, and he eventually wrote the *Prose Edda*, a guide to Viking mythology. Snorri was careful to point out that he did not believe in the old stories, and instead made the remarkably modern suggestion that most stories of the Viking "gods" were actually muddled fables about half-forgotten ancestors.

Snorri argued that cults could grow up around the tombs of famous or respected ancestors, and that if their descendants sought their aid in battle, and then won, it would create a loop of expectations and reinforcements. Those whose ancestors "failed" them would die out or be forgotten. Those whose ancestors were thought to have led them to victory after victory would live on to believe that these long-departed warriors had ever greater powers, eventually elevating them to godlike status.

Descendants of Gods?

Snorri was not the only writer to suggest that Viking "gods" were garbled references to real people. The medieval *Historia Norwegiae* mentions two gods in a family list that stretches from the time of legends to the first "king" of Norway. The catalog of kings also demonstrates a series of bizarre deaths typical of Vikings, including several allusions to human sacrifice:

Ingvi, from Sweden, ancestor of the Ynglings
Father of Njord, who was worshipped as a sea god
Father of Frey, who was worshipped as a fertility god
Father of Fjolnir, who drowned in a vat of mead
Father of Svegdir, who followed a dwarf into a mountain and was never seen again
Father of Vanlandi, who was suffocated by a demon in his sleep
Father of Visburr, who was burned alive by his own sons
Father of Domaldi, who was sacrificed by the Swedes as a harvest offering
Father of Dagr, who was killed in battle with the Danes
Father of Alrekr, who was beaten to death with a bridle by his own brother
Father of Hogni, who was hanged from a tree by his own wife
Father of Ingjald, killed by his own brother
Father of Jorundr, captured and hanged by the Danes
Father of Aun, who lived so long that he lived on milk for his last nine years
Father of Egill, whose kingdom was briefly usurped by a slave
Father of Ottar, killed by his own brother
Father of Adils, who fell from his horse and died
Father of Eysteinn, who was burned alive with his men by the Goths
Father of Yngvar, who died fighting in the Baltic Sea
Father of Braut Onund, who was killed by his brother
Father of Ingjald, who was burned alive in his feasting hall
Father of Olaf, who ruled peacefully and "died full of days"
Father of Halfdan, who died of old age
Father of Eysteinn, who drowned at sea
Father of Halfdan the Stingy, who had gold but not food
Father of Guthroth, who was the Hunting King
Father of Halfdan the Black, killed by his own wife
Father of Harald Fairhair, first historical king of Norway

Snorri also wrote the massive *Heimskringla* ("The Circle of the World"), a history of the kings of Norway during the Viking Age, which included anecdotes, poems, songs, and stories. Some of the stories were reported from his own family, since some of his own ancestors were eyewitnesses to the great events in Viking history.

56

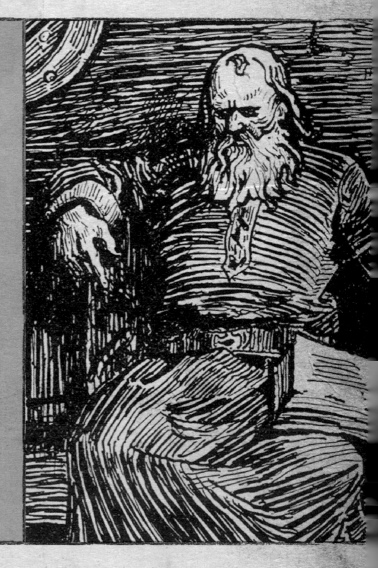

The Forgotten Sagas

Although Snorri compiled and edited vast numbers of local legends and stories, the chance remains that elements may have crept in from the myths of other cultures. Tales of the Viking Age were not the only sagas available to him in medieval Iceland. Books of the era also include Alexander's Saga, *which told the life of Alexander the Great;* Breta Sögur *and* Merlinusspá, *which were retellings of British legend, particularly tales of King Arthur;* Riddarasögur, *which featured French tales of knights and chivalry;* Trójumanna Saga, *recounting Greek legends of the fall of Troy; and* Rómerverja Saga, *based largely on the Roman historians Sallust and Lucan. Although Icelandic reading materials are usually thought of as pagan, they also included* Kristni Saga, *which concentrated on Bible stories and the history of Christianity; and* Leidarvisir *("Sign-Posts"), a guide book for pilgrims hoping to travel to the Holy Land. The existence of these sources may explain many points of similarity between what are assumed to be "Viking" legends and legends of the rest of Europe.*

The Death of Snorri

In later life, Snorri became involved in an attempted rebellion to free Iceland from Norwegian rule, and was murdered at his home in Reykholt. His last words, "Don't strike!" were initially regarded by local Icelanders as cowardly, and not befitting a man who had written so much about Vikings calmly staring death in the face. Later, commentators observed that his actual words were closer to "Thou shalt not kill," and that Snorri the Christian commentator was dying as he had lived.

His Icelandic neighbors, however, still clung to an element of the old lore. His ghost is said to haunt the place to this day.

57

Above. A page from Heimskringla, *one of Snorri's legacies*

VIKING MYTHS

Viking mythology gives us a chance to see the raiders as they saw themselves, a glimpse of the way they thought and the way they saw the world. It shows us that the Vikings saw the world as a constant war against trouble, born out of chaos, and doomed to end in destruction.

The Creation of the World

It was Time's morning,
When there nothing was;
Nor sand, nor sea,
Nor cooling billows.
Earth there was not,
Nor heaven above.
The Ginnungagap was,
But grass nowhere.
—The Elder Edda

58

In the beginning, there was nothing in the universe but two extremes. Severe, unbearable heat lay in one direction, and crushing, icy cold in another. They were separated by the great void of Ginnungagap, but somewhere in the middle, the ice met fire and the fire met ice, and something began to melt.

The first creatures were Ymir, first of the frost giants, and Audumla the cow. The cow licked at salty ice, unfreezing still more creatures, including the first god Buri. Buri and a giantess became the parents of Bor, the father of Odin and his two brothers Vili and Ve (Will and Woe).

The three brothers killed Ymir the giant, using his body to form the materials of our world. His blood soaked the universe and drowned all but two of the giants. It settled to become the waters of the oceans and lakes, while Ymir's bones became mountains and his flesh became the soil. His skull formed the dome of the sky, while pieces of ancient fires formed the sun and stars.

Odin and his three brothers divided the universe into three. The icy cold of Jotunheim was the new land of the giants. Asgard was the dwelling place of the gods. And in the middle was Midgard. Finding an ash tree and an elm tree on the shoreline, the gods created the first man, Ask, and the first woman, Embla.

The World Tree

Yggdrasil, the World Tree, held up the sky. Its roots rested in Asgard, Jotunheim, and Nifl-heim, the cold world of the dead. The gods met in council each morning at the base of the tree, near the Well of Fate.

Holding up the Sky?

Stories of Yggdrasil the World Tree may owe something to earlier religions of sky worship. The ancient Saxons were said to worship Irminsul, the "pillar that held up heaven," and there are references in Finnish mythology to something called a sampo, which may have originally been a similar "world tree."

Yggdrasil may even be a reference to the sky—its "trunk" being the Milky Way visible in the night sky. There are references in Viking legend to an eagle in its branches and a snake in its roots that send insulting messages to each other via a talkative squirrel. Such stories may have begun as a device to help Vikings remember the patterns of stars in the sky, and may still be preserved in some otherwise unintelligible designs on rune stones and shamanic drums from Lapland.

The Norns

Near the roots of the tree in Asgard was the Well of Fate, which is the home of the three Norns: Urd, Skuld, and Verdandi. Variously described as the spirits of Fate, Being, and Necessity (or Past, Present, and Future), these three mysterious women spin thread to make a tapestry of all life. Each person's life is a thread woven by the Norns—we are born when they weave it into the tapestry, and we die when it is tied and cut off. The Norns were said to visit every newborn baby in order to decide its fate.

As well as weaving or divining the fates of men, the Norns care for the Yggdrasil: it is their job to water the tree, to smear its ancient bark with soothing mud, and to scare off the animals that try to nibble on it.

From History to Myth

By the end of the Viking Age, those descendants who had become Christians, particularly in Iceland, began to rationalize early Viking legends and search for real-world parallels. Snorri Sturluson suggested that the Aesir (the family of Odin) and the Vanir (ancient fertility gods) were not gods at all, but wandering tribes from Asia who came to Scandinavia in the past and conquered the people who were already there. Fireside tales of their exploits were confused over the centuries and became fantastic stories of super-powered gods who coexist in an uneasy peace with other races such as the giants, dwarves, and elves.

Giants

The giants were the earliest inhabitants of the world, and inhabited Jotunheim, or "Giant-Home." Jotunheim is a region in modern Norway, but it has only gained its name relatively recently. We therefore cannot know where the historical Giant-Home may have been. The word *Jotun* (plural: Jotnar) did not originally mean "giant" at all, but was simply the name of a particular group who came to be associated with the icy, dangerous majesty of towering mountain peaks. Several gods had "giantesses" as wives or mothers.

60

Dwarves

Odin and the other gods often traded with the dwarves—cunning small men who live beneath mountains and who possess great skills at mining and working metals. Most of the gods' weapons and artifacts were of dwarf manufacture. The dwarves also had skills in brewing, and were able to brew ale that would heal wounds.

Elves

Viking myths are less specific about the "elves," a race that sometimes supplied bedmates to Viking gods. Elves were split into two classes: the "light" elves were similar to the gods themselves; the "dark" elves were similar to dwarves, and dwelt beneath the mountains. Alfheim ("Elf-Home") is thought to have originally referred to a region just north of modern-day Oslo.

THE VIKING "PANTHEON"

At the time he compiled his Viking stories, Snorri Sturluson thought of the Viking gods as a council of twelve, like the pantheon of Greco-Roman gods, or the twelve-strong jury that heard legal cases in medieval Iceland. However, it is often difficult to say exactly which god was responsible for what. Their job descriptions and powers do not divide up neatly, and it seems likely that the Viking "pantheon" was a relatively late invention.

In pre-Viking times, different villages, tribes, and families had different gods, and each regarded its own as the most powerful. Odin was particularly popular in Denmark, Sweden, and the Trondheim area of Norway, leading to the general view by outside observers that he was all-powerful. Thor was revered in the rest of Norway, and also in later Iceland, leading to his position in the pantheon as a major god, either as Odin's equal or his cherished son.

However, worshippers of Odin and Thor formed the bulk of the men who sailed abroad and became known as the Vikings. Place-names and artifacts suggest that many earlier gods were reduced to underling status by the Thor- and Odin-worshippers. Hence, in Viking mythology we have what appears to be an older, retired war-god, depicted as a wounded man, as well as half-forgotten fertility deities and local heroes. As Christianity began to take hold in the latter years of the Viking Age, Odin himself was increasingly portrayed as an old, injured man, his powers fading away.

Odin

Favored deity of Scandinavian warriors, Odin played a part in the creation of the world. Many elements of Odin's story seem based on rituals of death and human sacrifice. Odin put out one of his eyes in return for knowledge. He hanged himself from the branches of the World Tree to gain knowledge of the runes. His horse, Sleipnir, could run on sky and sea as easily as it could run on land. It also had eight legs, leading some to believe that "Odin's eight-legged horse" was a poetic reference to a coffin borne by four pallbearers.

Despite having only one eye, Odin knew all and saw all. His twin ravens, Hugin (Thought) and Munin (Memory), would fly out into the worlds of men and return to report the news of brave-fought battles or cowardly deeds.

61

Odin's weapon of choice was the magic spear Gungnir (Swayer), made for him by dwarf craftsmen. Once hurled in battle, it never missed, and its shadow was thought to confer defeat on those beneath it. This belief led to a Viking custom of hurling a spear over the heads of their enemies at the commencement of hostilities, in order to gain Odin's support in the battle to come.

The Names of Odin

Thanks to skalds' poetic allusions, legends, and anecdotes, Odin had over a hundred names and titles to the Vikings. He was known sometimes as the Father of Men, the All-Father, the Mighty God, the Blind One, the Author of Victory, the Spear God, the Blazing Eye, the Battle Screamer, Hang-Jaw, and the Wanderer. He is even sometimes known as Jolnir, the "Yule Figure"—an old bearded man who might arrive at a homestead in the middle of winter and ask for a place to stay. Food and lodging granted to this spirit of winter might bring great fortune to the locals, although dreadful calamity might befall them if they turned this disguised traveler away—a likely precursor of later centuries' Santa Claus.

62

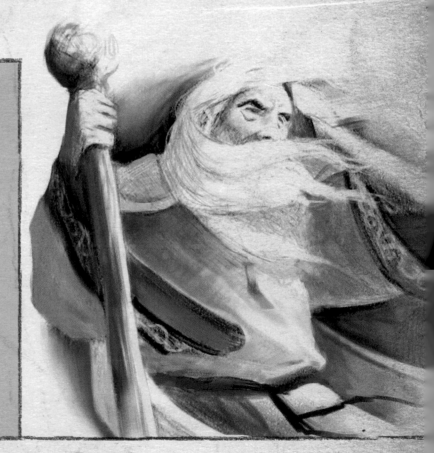

Gandalf

The author J. R. R. Tolkien once wrote that he based his depiction of Gandalf in The Lord of the Rings as an "Odinic wanderer"—a figure with divine powers now manifested as an old man. The name Gandalf ("Wand-elf") was originally borrowed by Tolkien from an Icelandic collection, the Elder Edda.

It may seem strange that Odin was regarded as a warrior and a poet, but religious leaders in the Viking Age and beyond were expected to memorize long catalogues of laws or deeds. Mastery of the runes, which also were sacred to Odin, could function as a form of code and an aid to memory. Also, we must remember that much of what we know about the Viking gods comes to us through the preserved stories of bards and skalds. These poets would have been sure to play up the nature of Odin as a generous host and lover of poetry, thus encouraging the Vikings they entertained to treat singers and poets with a greater degree of respect.

Odin's names reflect his status as a god, warrior, and wise leader, but also sometimes as a trickster, or deity that demands human sacrifice. He is also called the Lord of Ghosts and the Mound-Lord. In battle, he is particularly known for his association with two groups in particular: special warriors considered to be "blessed by Odin," and mythical female spirits considered to be his servants—the berserkers and the valkyries.

Odin, in his Saxon form Woden, gives his name to Wednesday in English.

63

The Viking Days of the Week

Sun's Day
Moon's Day
Tyr's Day
Odin's Day
Thor's Day
Freya's Day
Wash Day

Odin, the All-father

Berserkers

According to Viking belief, certain warriors might find themselves entering a terrible rage, or a "mist of Odin." These were considered to be the elite warriors of a Viking band, whose battle-rage permitted them to shrug off wounds and take on foes with impossible odds. The term by which they are most commonly known is *berserkir* (bear-shirts) although some sources refer to them as *ulfhednar* (wolfskins). Berserkers have become a fundamental part of the Viking mystique, although their standing, behavior, and role seems to have undergone major shifts during the Viking Age.

Initially, berserkers were simply the toughest, strongest warriors in a Viking band, prized for their prowess in battle, and doubtlessly described as "blessed by Odin" by timid poets hoping to stay on their good side. Such fighters may have been genuinely skilled, or more possibly described in modern terms as psychopaths who actively sought out conflict situations. Since the berserkers often occupied a "place of honor" at the prow of a ship or at the front line of a battle, they might even be described as the warriors who were foolhardy enough to be easily persuaded that their position was the best place to be!

Stories of the berserkers seem to confuse some of their abilities and behavior with that of shamans. Like Norse priests, the berserkers may have similarly used drugs or hallucinogenic plants to gain "Odin's blessing," which may also explain some saga accounts that describe them literally turning into wild animals, in imitation of the shape-shifting powers of legendary sorcerers.

64

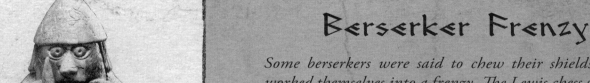

Berserker Frenzy

Some berserkers were said to chew their shields as they worked themselves into a frenzy. The Lewis chess set, made in Trondheim and found on the Shetland Islands, features a shield-chewing berserker among its pawns.

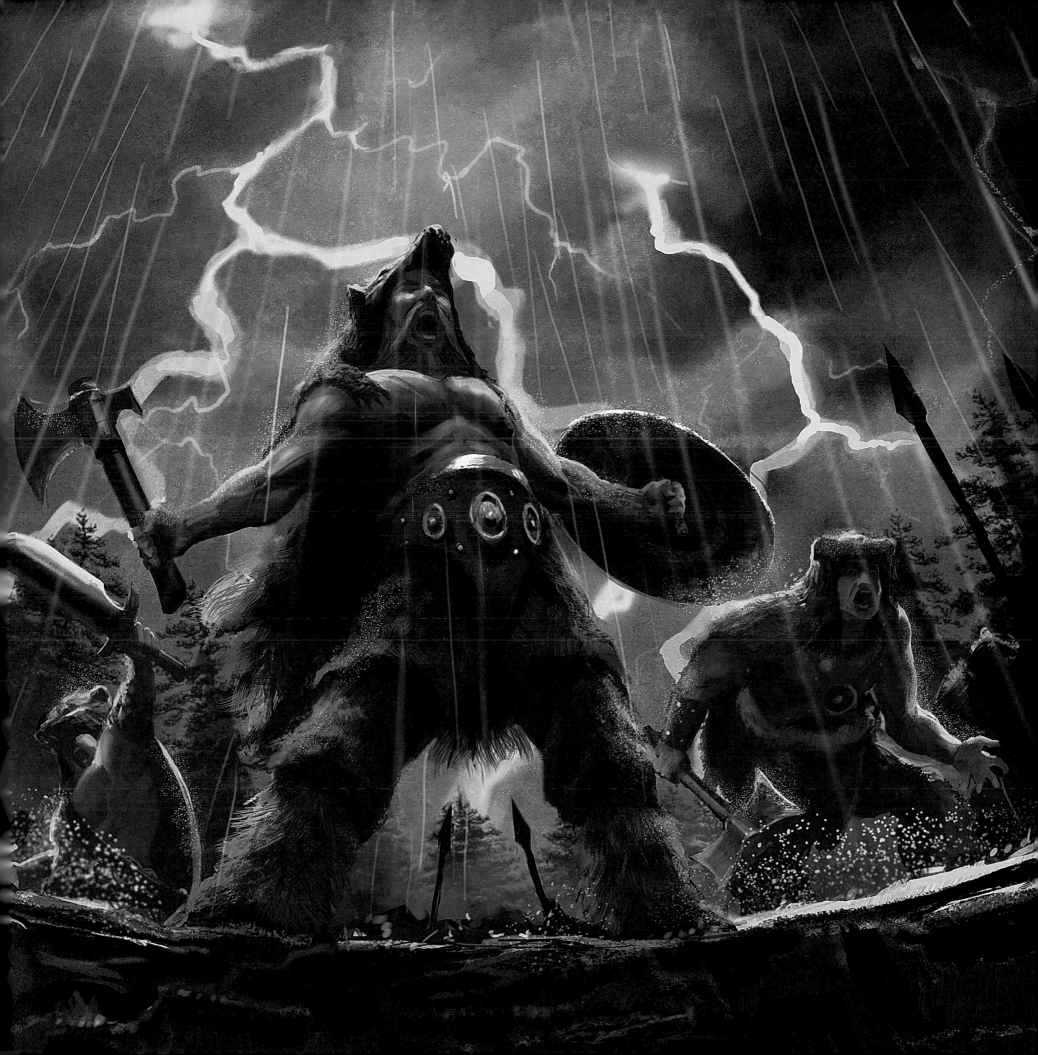

By the time of the Viking kings in the ninth century, there were references in the Norse king sagas to full platoons of berserkers in the service of certain leaders. Such warriors seem to have worn bearskins to add to their imposing presence, and may simply have been the best troops in a Norse leader's war-band.

Berserkers were honored largely by societies that were based on the principles of nomadic warriors. As the Vikings settled down and formed sedentary societies, or joined armies that required a more unified form of military discipline, the berserkers lost much of their brutish appeal. In the later Viking Age and beyond, references to berserkers change in tone. To Christian homesteaders in Iceland, with land to defend and jobs to do, "berserkers" were more likely to be outlaws or random murderers. In Icelandic sagas, berserkers often are depicted as as violent criminals who are dealt with by local heroes.

Valkyries

Odin's most famous servants were his legendary battle-maidens, the Choosers of the Slain, or *valkyrja*—known in English as Valkyries. The Valkyries were beautiful but terrifying spirit-women who would ride into battle with Odin in search of the bravest warriors. On Odin's order, the Valkyries would carry off the souls of the bravest warriors who fell in combat, and take them to Valhalla, Odin's Hall of the Slain.

At Valhalla, the Valkyries would welcome the new-fallen heroes with cups of the finest mead. Warriors would find themselves in the finest of feasting halls, roofed over with spears, and decorated with coats of armor and shields—and they would be sure to have their own swords from their grave burial. A great feast would begin, with more mead and meat, at which the drunken warriors and their beautiful female companions would be entertained by songs from Bragi, the god of poetry. Then, the warriors would pile out of Valhalla's 640 doors and fight each other. Any who were killed a second time could be brought back from the dead, until the end of the world, when Odin, his bravest Vikings, and the Valkyries (as shield-bearers) would make their final stand against the gods' mortal enemies, the giants.

One saga's reference to a vision before the Battle of Clontarf describes the Valkyries as horrific, bestial versions of the maidenly Norns, weaving a tapestry of fate, not with threads, but with bloody human entrails.

The Queen of Asgard

Although there were several goddess cults in ancient and medieval Scandinavia, detailed information on who those goddesses were is hard to find. The Vikings were largely interested in gods of battle, and there are only occasional references to those deities who might have been worshipped by women.

Frigg, sometimes called the wife of Odin, seems to have ruled over childbirth. Women who died while carrying or giving birth to a child were sacred to Frigg, and they were liable to be welcomed to her sacred halls in much the same way as her husband welcomed men who died in battle.

Frigg, or possibly her "younger form" Freya, gives her name to Friday in English.

67

Brynhild

The most famous Valkyrie is Brynhild ("Bright Battle") from the Volsunga Saga. Although Odin promises victory to his loyal worshipper Hjalmgunnar, Brynhild "chooses" Hjalmgunnar as one of the slain and causes his death. In punishment, Brynhild was left in an eternal sleep, in a hall surrounded by a wall of fire. She was rescued by the hero Sigurd, but she was later fooled into marrying Sigurd's brother-in-law. Vengefully arranging for Sigurd's death, Brynhild is unable to forgive herself, and throws herself onto his funeral pyre. The story later inspired Richard Wagner's opera The Valkyrie, in which the similarly named Brünnhilde commits a different crime against the gods, by bringing a woman, rather than a man, from a battlefield.

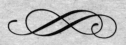 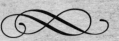

The God Of Thunder

Although Odin was the Lord of Hosts and the Father God, many Vikings identified more closely with his brawling son Thor, the God of Thunder. Such an attitude extended into the Christian Age, when one Icelandic woman once told a missionary that Thor, son of Odin, had challenged Jesus, son of the Christian God, to a duel, but that Christ had not shown up.

Thor was the deity responsible for incredible physical feats, weather both good and bad, the swearing of oaths, and thunder and lighting. With his red beard and his mighty hammer, he may have once been a fire god or god of blacksmiths, before his association with thunder and lightning. Statues of Thor may have had an iron nail driven into their forehead, from which sparks could be struck with a flint, in re-enactment of one of his mythical battles, but also for the kindling of a sacred fire.

68

Thor's Hammer

Thor's hammer, Mjöllnir, never missed its mark, even when thrown. Having struck its target, it would magically fly back into its wielder's hand. Vikings often wore a T-shaped hammer amulet as a symbol of their allegiance to the old gods. During the rise of Christianity, some jewelers had molds that could cast Christian crucifixes and pagan hammers in the same session.

Thor placed great value on his hammer, and would do anything to get it back. When the giant Thrym stole the hammer and held it for ransom until the beautiful goddess Freya gave herself to him, Thor disguised himself as Freya, only to throw off his wedding veil and slaughter the guests when the hammer was back in his possession.

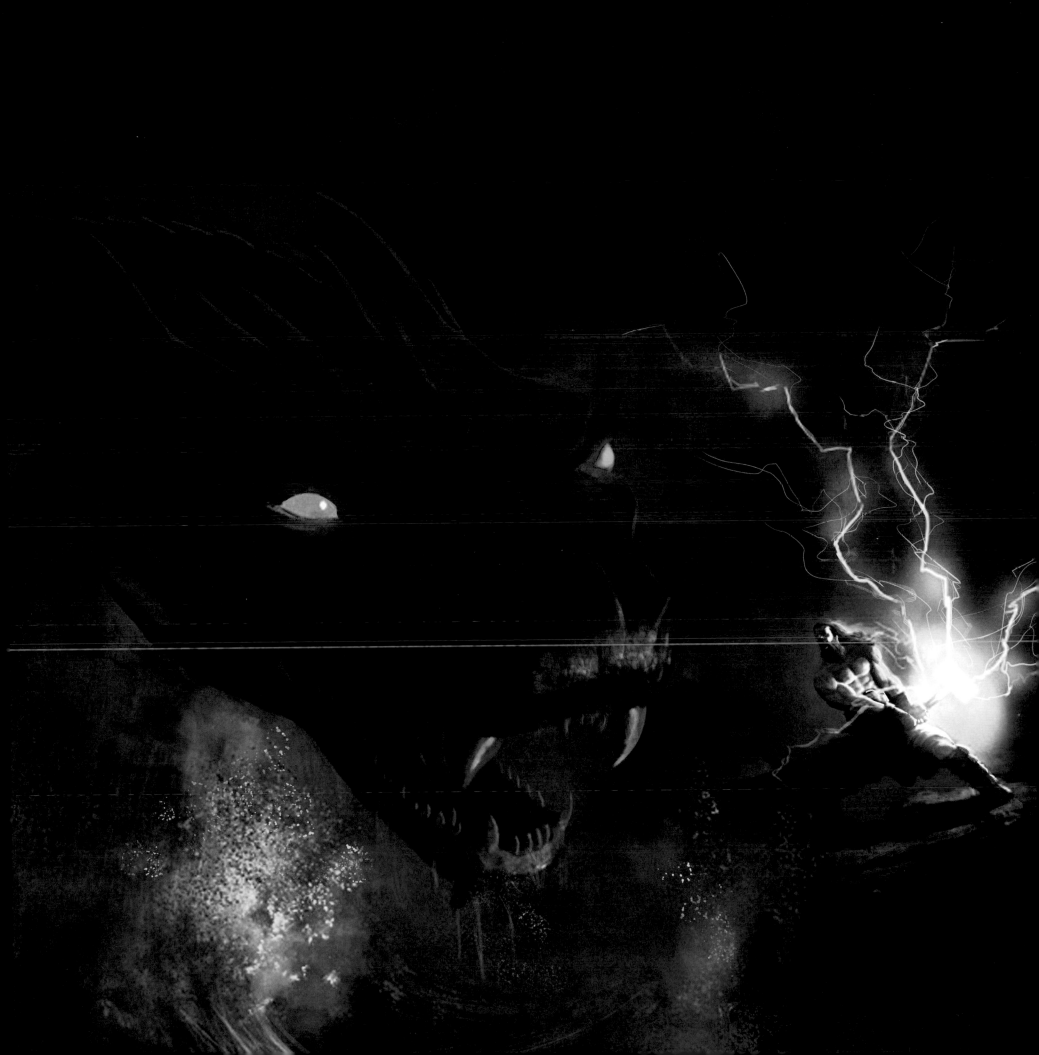

Thor was sometimes depicted riding in a chariot pulled by two goats. He could slaughter these goats for food and then use his hammer's powers to recall them to life. The rumbling of his chariot's wheels was said to be the sound of thunder in the sky. Some sort of ceremonial chariot may have been a feature of Thor's temple. Pulling this chariot in a circuit amounted to paying homage to Thor, and also to swearing an oath under his protection.

The Stone in Thor's Head

In a fight with a stone-headed giant called Mist-Calf, Thor threw his hammer at the same time that the giant threw a huge whetstone. The hammer shattered the stone, although one of its fragments was embedded in Thor's forehead. He asked a sorceress to help him remove it, but she became distracted by his story about the time he met her husband and threw her husband's toe into the sky. She never finished casting her spell. The stone remained in Thor's head ever after, and may have inspired part of a ceremonial striking of fire at Scandinavian ceremonies.

70

Legends of Thor often center on his capacity for food and drink. In a series of contests against giants, Thor was initially ashamed that his hammer blows could not hurt a giant, his drinking could not empty a drinking-horn, and his strength was not sufficient to lift a humble cat. In a final trial, he was unable to defeat an old woman in a wrestling match. It was only later revealed that Thor's challenges were unwinnable: his hammer blows had smashed craters in a mountain side, his drinking had threatened to empty the sea (and create low tide), and the "cat" had really been the head of the Midgard Serpent itself, a giant snake that encircled the entire planet. Finally, his wrestling opponent was Old Age itself, which brought down every single enemy in the end, even a god.

Thor gives his name to Thursday in English.

THE WATCHMAN AT THE RAINBOW BRIDGE

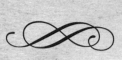 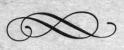

Heimdall was the watchman of the gods, blessed with the ability to see further than any man, and with ears so sensitive that they could hear the sound of grass or sheep's wool growing. Heimdall lived by the side of Bifrost, the great Rainbow Bridge, and kept constant watch in case of a giant attack.

Gjallarhorn

In an emergency, Heimdall could blow upon Gjallarhorn (the "Echoing Horn"), which he kept hidden amid the roots of Yggdrasil, the World Tree. Gjallarhorn was said to be loud enough to be heard in "all the worlds"—leading to inevitable comparisons with the "last trumpet" said to herald the end of the world in the biblical book Revelations. *If Heimdall ever had cause to blow his horn, it would be a sign that the last battle between the gods and giants was about to begin.*

71

The God Who Was Tuesday

Norse mythology recognized another war-god, in the form of Tyr, thought to be a corrupted form of the Germanic sky-god Tiwaz. In pre-Viking times, Tyr was the only war-god, comparable to Mars in Roman accounts. By the time of the Vikings, his worshippers had largely been defeated or supplanted by Odin-worshippers, leading to Tyr's reimagining as a son of Odin.

Perhaps in memory of some forgotten conflict between tribes, Tyr is depicted as a brave god who bears a permanent reminder of his most famous battle. It was Tyr who volunteered to chain the savage Fenris Wolf, using the magical chain Gleipnir, which was made by dwarves from the stealth of a cat's footstep, the strength of a mountain's roots, the delicacy of a woman's beard, the lightness of a bird's spit, and the toughness of a bear's sinews. Tyr successfully chained the wolf, thereby preventing it from getting free and eating the sun, but in the process, the wolf bit off his hand.

Tyr, in his Saxon form Tiw, gives his name to Tuesday in English.

The Vanir

A mysterious feature of Viking gods can be seen in what appears to be two rival clans among them. The Aesir of Asgard are the family of Odin, and they appear to live in a state of relative peace with an earlier group of gods they supplanted.

This earlier group, the Vanir, seem to have been the fertility gods of earlier inhabitants of Scandinavia, perhaps farmers' deities reduced in status after the arrival of a violent new warring class who promoted the worship of more powerful gods like Odin and Thor. Their chief god was Njord, a god ruling fertility and the sea. However, by the time of the Viking Age, only two of his children remained within the Norse imagination.

Freya

Freya was a goddess of love and sex, who traveled in a chariot pulled by cats. She was married to a god who is rarely mentioned, although his name is usually recorded as Od or Oth. He may have been an earlier variant on Odin, and she on Frigg. Since her husband was frequently absent, the frustrated Freya would weep tears of gold—in this regard, she may have originally been a harvest-bride, whose "golden tears" were actually ears of corn, shed for the annual death of her harvest-husband.

Freya was divinely beautiful, and often the subject of proposals from love-struck giants, although she never accepted their offers. She was subjected to a series of allegations about her licentious behavior, and once was even accused of sleeping with her own brother, Frey. Her most famous possession was Brisingamen, the "necklace of bright fire." To acquire this golden artifact, she spent a night with each of the dwarves who made it—a deed which only added to her risqué reputation among the gods.

When Snorri chronicled the histories and beliefs of the Vikings, he noted that Freya was "the only god that yet lived," implying that she was still worshipped in some corners of the Scandinavian world, long after the coming of Christianity.

The Twin Gods

Long before the Viking Age, the Roman author Tacitus recorded that barbarian tribes worshipped twin gods, whose priests dressed as women. This may have been the distant origin of several twin-cults across Scandinavia by the time of the Vikings, of which Frey and Freya were the most recognizable to Snorri when he wrote about the "old gods." Thor's mother, Fjorgynn, seems to have had a male twin, Fjorgyn. Where Norway meets Finland, local clans worshipped twin girls, Thorgerda and Irpa. In Sweden, there was once a cult that recognized twin gods of hunting and skiing, Ull and Ulla. In Denmark, twin sea gods were possibly known as Njord and Nerthus.

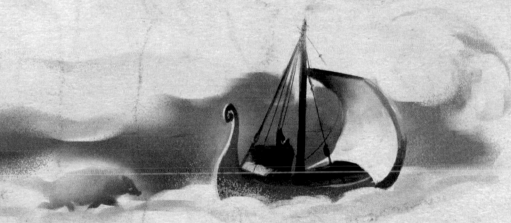

Frey

Freya's brother, Frey, was another fertility god, with power over the sun, the rain, and the fruitfulness of the earth. He was also the mythical ancestor of the Ynglings—the clan that would eventually become the ruling royal house of Sweden. Frey's magical possessions included a ship that could fold up in his pocket, but also open out to be large enough to contain all the gods; and Gullinbursti ("Golden Bristles"), a wild boar that glowed in the dark.

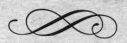
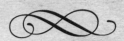

THE TRICKSTER GOD

Strangest of all the gods is Loki, who is recorded as one of the Aesir of Asgard, even though his parents were giants. Loki is an often unwelcome immigrant in the court of the Viking gods, and is unique among the deities in that he does not appear to have had any worshippers. Place-names throughout Scandinavia and beyond point to places sacred to Viking gods—groves of Thor, clearings of Odin, hills of Frey—but nowhere does there appear a temple to Loki. Instead, he is a prankster among the gods, always to be found at the center of trouble.

Loki is unpredictable and dangerous—like fire, he is useful when kept under control, but dangerous when left to his own devices. He is also responsible, sometimes inadvertently, for the creation of many of the new monsters that plague the Viking gods in their most famous battles.

Loki is the father of Hel, the Norse goddess of the underworld, as well as father of the terrible giant Fenris Wolf and the massive Midgard Serpent that encircles the entire globe with its tail in its mouth. Loki is also a shape-shifter, able to turn into a flea when mischief calls him to steal Freya's necklace, or into a salmon or a seal when he needs to make a quick getaway. Loki is also bizarrely the "mother" of Odin's horse, since Loki turned himself into a mare in order to lure a stallion away from the building of the walls of Asgard, and in so doing became pregnant with the eight-legged Sleipnir.

74

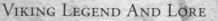

Ottar's Ransom

Loki's run of bad luck began when he stole treasure from the dwarf Andvari. Andvari lived beneath a waterfall, and could transform himself into a fish. Loki caught Andvari with a net, and made him give up all of his treasure, including the beautiful golden ring Andvarinaut. Andvari cursed the ring so that it would bring misfortune to any that owned it. Sure enough, Loki soon killed an otter by the riverside, only to discover that it was actually Ottar, the son of a local king temporarily turned into beast form. Loki was obliged to pay reparations to the king by covering his son with gold. The ring was required to close the last gap in the pile of gold. The king, however, was later killed for the ring by his own son, Fafnir. Fafnir turned into a dragon, and was killed by the hero Sigurd, who took the ring and gave it to his Valkyrie love Brynhilde, hence causing her own death when he left her.

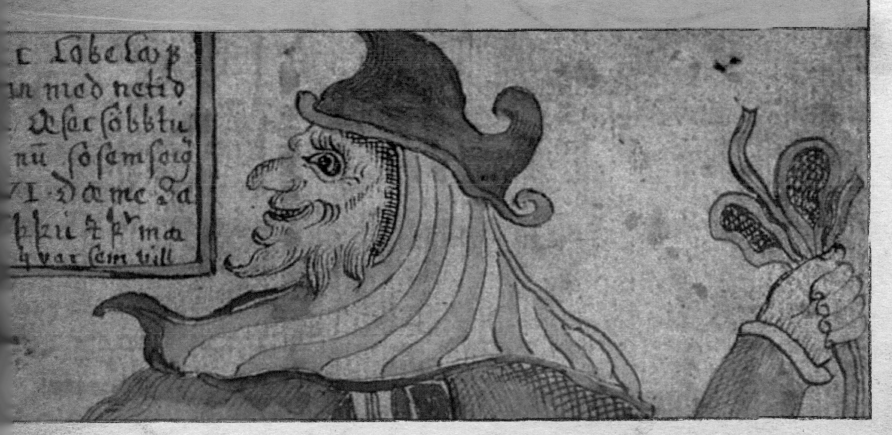

Above: Loki illustration from an eighteenth-century Icelandic manuscript

Loki's Jealousy

Loki took his mischief too far in the case of Balder, the young son of Odin and Frigg, who was loved by all the gods. Balder is described as a kind and gentle figure, a sun-god whose story seems interlaced with later additions from Christian stories of sacrifice and martyrdom, as well as the Greek legends of Achilles. Frigg loved her mild-mannered son Balder so much that she gained assurances from every single thing in the natural world that he would not be harmed. Balder's invulnerability became something of a sport with the gods, who would sometimes hurl objects at him to watch them bounce off.

Loki, however, found a loophole. Frigg had neglected to gain any assurances from mistletoe, which she had forgotten because it was a parasite that grew upon other plants. Jealous of Balder's standing with the other gods, Loki convinced the blind god Hoder to throw a dart at Balder. Since the dart was made of mistletoe, it penetrated Balder's magical defenses and killed him.

The gods were so grief-stricken at the loss of Balder that Odin sent his son Hermod down to the underworld to plead for his return. Hel, the goddess of the underworld, offered to bring Balder back to life if every living thing would shed a tear. However, a single ancient giantess (really Loki in disguise) refused, causing Balder to remain in the underworld.

76

Another Balder Myth?

The medieval writer Saxo Grammaticus, in his History of the Danes, *recounted a completely different version of the story, in which Balder and Hoder were human heroes, rivals for the hand of the maiden Nanna. Raised by Valkyries, Balder was fed poisoned food from an early age, thus developing great invulnerability. Hoder mortally wounded Balder with a stolen magic sword, leading Odin to sire a human child, Boe, conceived for the sole purpose of avenging the death of Balder. Saxo's story is radically different from Snorri's, not in the least for its concentration on purportedly real locations—he stops the narrative to note the continued existence of a spring where Balder once drank, and even pinpoints Balder's burial mound, in which some unlucky Vikings had almost drowned when trying to rob it. Notably, several Viking sagas mention a magic sword that went by the name of Mistletoe.*

The Binding of Loki

Fearing for his life, Loki fled the vengeful gods, transforming himself into a salmon. The gods caught him with a net that he himself had designed and tried to burn. In apparent imitation or ritual suggestion of a gutted fish, he was tied across a flat stone, held down by one of his children's entrails. There, he was doomed to stay until the end of the world, with poison dripping into his eyes from the mouth of a snake above his head. His loyal wife stayed by his side to catch the poison in a bowl, but every time she turned aside to empty it, poison would fall on Loki's eyes, and his writhings would cause earthquakes.

77

A Finnish Connection?

One reason Loki does not appear to have any Viking worshippers is that he may not have even been a Viking god. His name bears some similarity to Louhi, an ancient Finnish goddess of the underworld, who may have been confused in later times with his daughter. The Finnish word for salmon is lohi, the same creature into which Loki was able to transform himself.

Above: Louhi, Finnish Goddess of the Underworld *by Akseli Gallen-Kallela*

RAGNAROK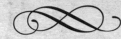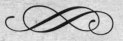

*Brothers will fight together
And become each other's bane;
Sisters' children
Their sib shall spoil
Hard is the world,
Sensual sins grow huge.
There are axe-ages, sword-ages—
Shields are cleft in twain—
There are wind-ages, wolf-ages,
Ere the world falls dead.*

—*Voluspa*

The Viking Age spanned an important event in the Christian calendar: the arrival of the year 1000, which many thought might herald the end of the world. Indeed, some Christian writers even thought the Vikings themselves might be one of the signs that the end of the world was near. One of the main mentions of the end of the world is the Prophecy of the Seeress (Voluspa), written some time around the year 1000.

Even before Snorri came to compile his book of Viking myths, stories about the Viking apocalypse had either been mingled with older Vanir-god influenced tales of rebirth, or perhaps even Bible stories. Evidence of such parallel mythologizing can be found all over the Viking world, in places such as Andreas on the Isle of Man, where a Christian cross bears a carving of Odin and the Fenris Wolf.

According to Viking tradition, the first sign of the end of the world is the Fimbulvintr ("The Great Winter"), in which no summer comes for three whole years. A mighty earthquake shakes the World Tree itself, and every bound creature in the world shakes off its fetters, including both Loki, who escapes his eternal torment to raise a giant army, and the Fenris Wolf, which runs into the sky and eats the sun.

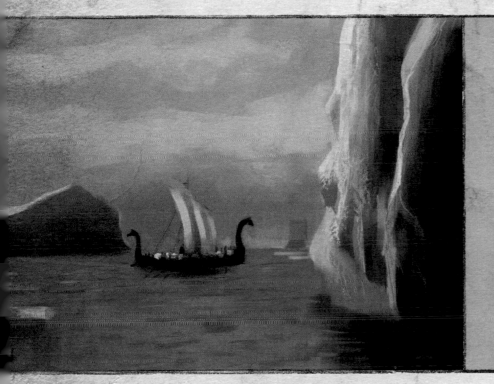

The Little Ice Age

At the time Snorri wrote his accounts, there would have been a keen interest in tales of a Great Cold, as the Earth was demonstrably getting colder. The late Middle Ages saw the onset of a "Little Ice Age," which increased the number of icebergs in the North Atlantic, and effectively cut off the Greenlanders from Europe. Iceland stayed in contact with Europe, but the journey became much more hazardous, until the Earth began warming up again in the eighteenth century.

79

Other Wolves

Other Viking myths ignore Fenris, and suggest that the sun will be eaten by two other wolves, Skoll and Hati, who chase the sun across the sky every day, and finally catch it as the coming cold causes it to slow down.

As the seas rise up, the evil frost giants set sail in Naglfar, a ship made from the fingernails of corpses, steered by Loki. He leads her undead warriors out of the underworld, and Surtr, leader of the fire giants, charges across Bifrost the Rainbow Bridge. Heimdall, watchman of the gods, blows his horn, and the final battle begins.

Nail Farer

Naglfar, the ship of the frost giants, was considered to be under construction until the end of the world. Vikings always buried their dead with trimmed nails, on the understanding that it would therefore take the giants longer to complete their ship, thus delaying the end of the world.

80

The Last Battle

In the last battle, the enemies of the gods approach from all directions. The Midgard Serpent rises from the waters, causing the waves to churn and thrash against the shores. The fire giants advance from the south, their leader Surtr waving a sword made of flames. Loki's frost giants will advance from the north, as if the elements themselves are closing in on the narrow band of life between them. Battle finally is waged on the icy plain of Vigrid. The first to fall is Frey, who charges Surtr the fire giant, but is cut down because he has foolishly lent his best sword to his servant. Thor smites the Midgard Serpent with his hammer, but drowns in its poison. Odin dies in the jaws of the Fenris Wolf, but Odin's son Vidar, whose mighty shoe is made of the off-cuts of all men's footwear, places his foot on the wolf's lower jaw and rips it apart. Tyr, the one-handed god of war, dies, even as he deals the death blow to Garm, the hound of hell.

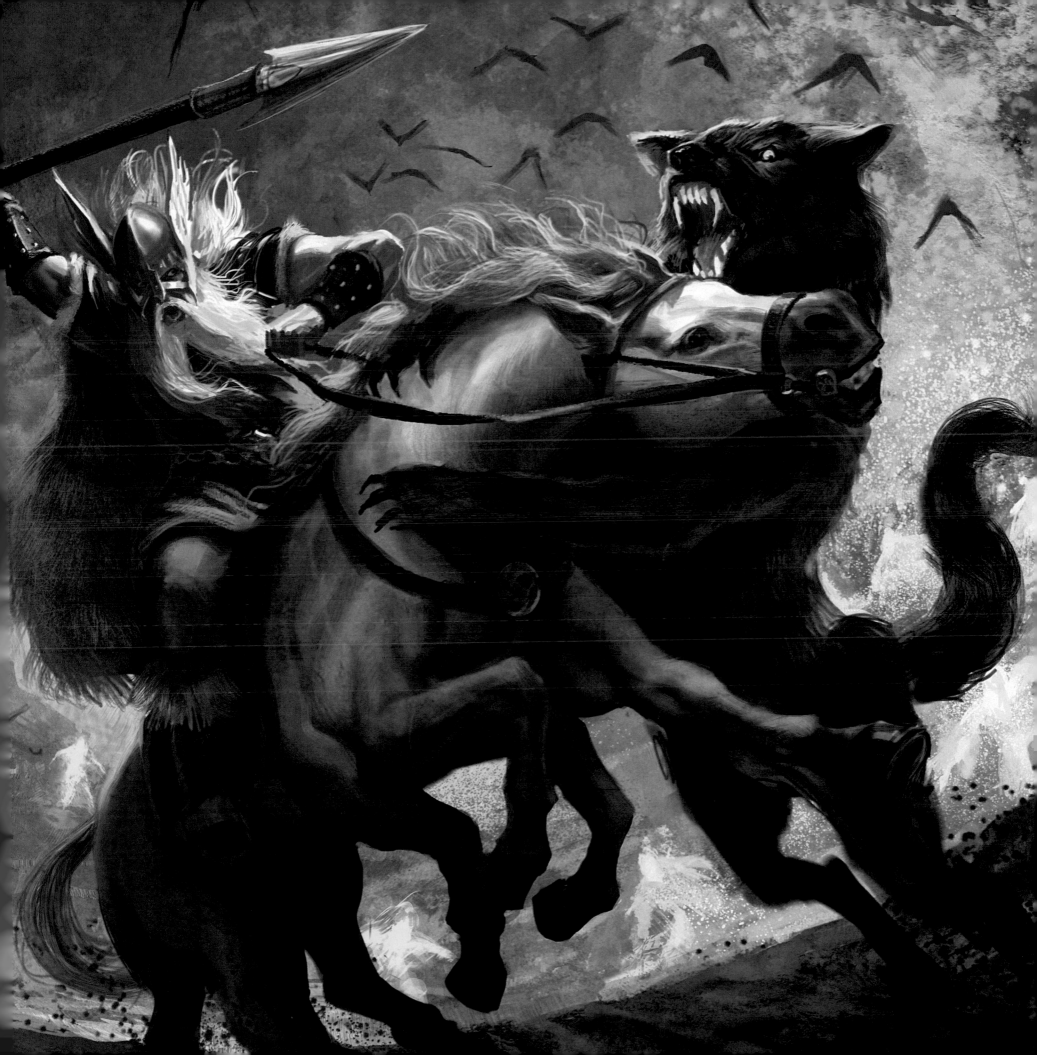

The Beginning of the World

The prophecies of Norse seers noted that there were other heavens and other underworlds, and the dead gods of the Norse world would live on in a new paradise. Meanwhile, Balder, the innocent victim of Loki's schemes, would survive to become the god of a new order, and a man and a woman would be found safe and well in a forest. Their children would repopulate the world.

The last words of the Prophecy of the Seeress suggest that there is something else far more powerful than the gods of old: a Great Godhead, whose arrival heralds the "doom of the world," but only in order to replace it with something better. The last sight in the prophecy, however, is Nithhoggr, a "corpse-devouring" dragon, swooping onto the battlefield for a grim finale.

82

A Translation Error?

While writing his version of the end of the world, Snorri appears to have accidentally confused Ragnarök, "the fate/doom of the reigning powers," with Ragnarøkkr, "the twilight of the gods." It is this latter version that is more famous today, through its appearance in Wagner's opera Götterdämmerung, "The Twilight of the Gods."

Surtr's Isle

Tales of fire crashing into ice were particularly meaningful for Icelanders such as Snorri, who lived in a world of extreme cold, over hot springs and volcanoes that occasionally broke through to ground level. In 1963, Iceland gained its newest and most southern land when a volcano burst through the sea floor and created a new island. The Icelandic government named it Surtsey—"Surtr's Isle"—after the leader of the fire giants. A second island, called Jolnir after one of the names of Odin, appeared later, but was swiftly eroded back below sea level.

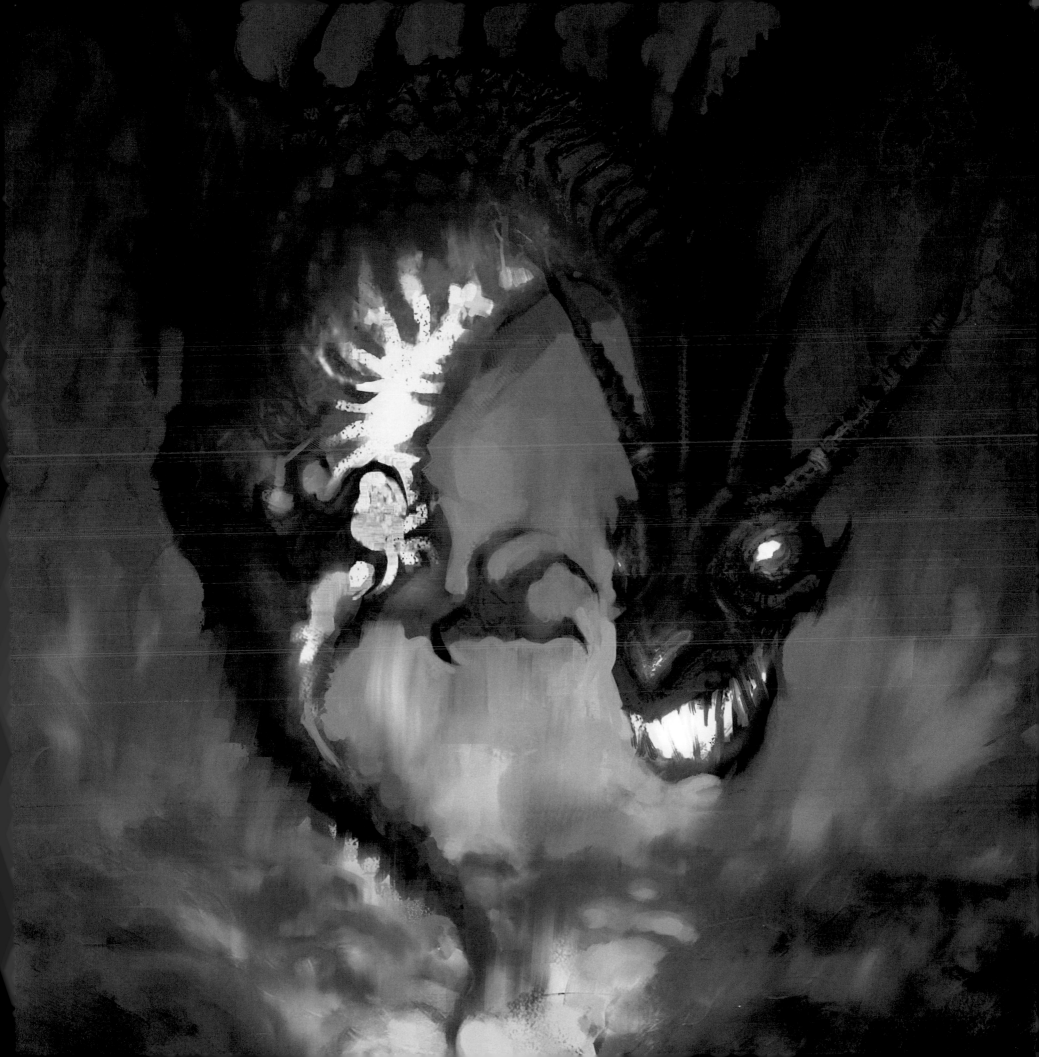

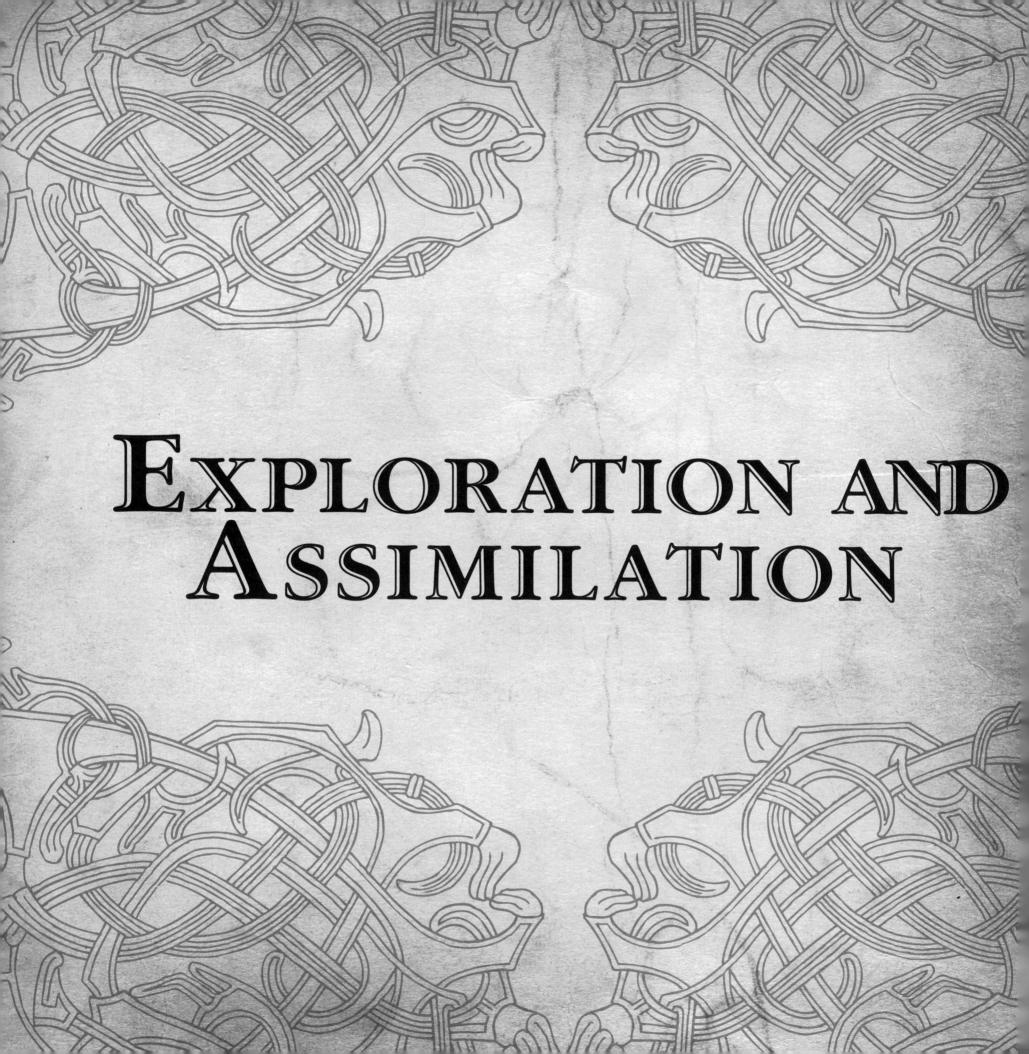

Exploration and Assimilation

FROM RUS TO RUSSIANS

Not only did the Vikings spread out into Western Europe—while Ireland, the British Isles, and northern France fell to raiders from Norway and Denmark, their Swedish cousins turned their attentions eastward, across the Baltic.

According to evidence from graves in what is now Latvia and Poland, Scandinavians had been trading and sailing across the Baltic Sea for hundreds of years before the beginning of the Viking Age, mainly to collect furs to sell in Western Europe. Norse sailors used the lakes and rivers of Eastern Europe, carrying their ships across the short distances between them. By using this portaging method, the Vikings were able to reach all the way down to the Black Sea and the Caspian Sea. The new arrivals were called Rus—possibly derived from a local word for rowers. Without offshore islands to use as bases, the Vikings were forced to set up inland trading quarters on river islands or in small forts, leading to a new Scandinavian term for the region Gardariki—"the place of fortified towns."

The Rus were always in the minority. Although a few settled in fortified towns, they were outnumbered by local peoples, and many of their descendants soon took on Slavic names, probably because they had local women as their mothers or nurses.

85

Rurik

The legendary first ruler of the Rus was Rurik, a Scandinavian who was supposedly invited into the region by feuding local people. According to local legend, Rurik and his two brothers pacified the region, although it is unclear whether they were truly invited in, invaded, or arrived as mercenaries before seizing control for themselves. Rurik's son Helgi (called Oleg in the local language) was told by a prophet that his horse would cause his death. Accordingly, he never rode it, and when it died, Oleg went to laugh at it, and was bitten by a lethal snake. If Oleg existed, he is more likely to have been killed in a battle with tribesmen in the south.

By the 830s, the Rus had traveled so far to the southeast that they were able to establish contact with Muslim traders on the banks of the Caspian Sea. The Islamic world was rich in silver and hungry for slaves, and the Vikings obliged by seizing prisoners in their European raids and then selling them to the Muslims. Graves found in Sweden contain literally thousands of Islamic dirhams, or silver coins. The Vikings called the Islamic world Serkland, which translates as either "Land of the Saracens" or "Land of Silk."

Reaching the Black Sea and Caspian Sea was a long and difficult journey, along rivers flanked by hostile barbarian tribes, and through the treacherous waters of numerous waterfalls and rapids.

The Holmgard Expedition

Between 1994 and 1995, the replica Viking ship Aifur *successfully sailed from the Baltic Sea to the Black Sea. The ship wintered in the former Rus town of Novgorod, as the original traders might have done. The distance covered from Sweden to the Ukraine was a total of 1,833 miles. The voyage of the* Aifur *proved the feasibility of sailing a Viking vessel along the route, although several rivers are demonstrably lower in modern times compared to the Middle Ages, and could not be sailed today. The crew also fashioned wooden wheels on a riverbank, attached them to their ship as a makeshift cart, and literally wheeled their vessel to the next stream.*

Trade did not always go well for the Vikings on the Caspian Sea. If the Muslim merchants were not buying, the Vikings might find themselves hundreds of miles from home with nothing to show for it. On such occasions, they sometimes went raiding on the shores of the Caspian Sea, although few of their raids were successful. Late in the tenth century, the supply of Muslim silver began to dry up, tempting many Vikings to turn their attentions back to Europe, or to new pastures in Ireland or Iceland.

Vikings and Muslims

In the year 922, the Muslim writer Ahmad Ibn Fadlan met with Rus traders at Itil on the north shore of the Caspian Sea. He was disgusted by their personal habits, and described them "as stupid as donkeys," but was impressed by their "perfect bodies." He also noted that they drank alcohol "night and day," to such a degree that one died with a cup still in his hand. The men that Ibn Fadlan met were selling slave girls snatched from parts of Europe, and the men were already showing signs of mixing Viking ways with manners and customs derived from Slavic peoples. He also witnessed a Viking funeral, in which a dead chieftain was interred with a slave girl who had volunteered to be killed to accompany him into the afterlife. Ibn Fadlan's account ends with the leader's ship being set on fire by his followers, burning the bodies inside it. Such cremations seem to have been common throughout the Viking world.

87

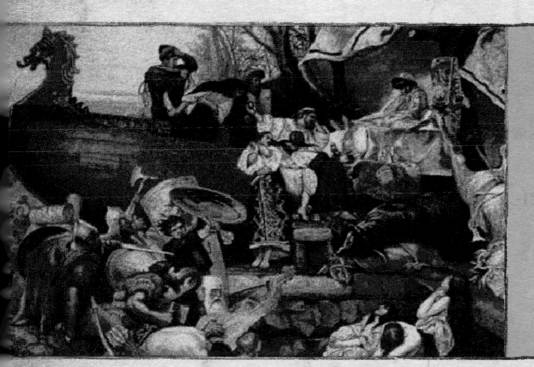

Up-Helly-Aa

The type of funeral described by Ibn Fadlan is recreated every year, without actual dead bodies, as part of the Up-Helly-Aa festival in the Shetland Islands, where a replica Viking ship is set on fire and pushed out to sea.

Above: Burial of Igor the Old by Heinrich Semiradski

MIKLAGARD

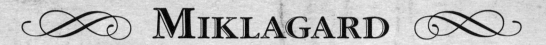

Far to the south, on the coasts of the Black Sea, was a city that the Vikings regarded as the richest in the world. They called it Miklagard, the "Great City," but its own inhabitants called it Constantinople.

Constantinople was the center of the Byzantine Empire, the eastern remnant of the great empire of Rome. Although there were several raids by Rus Vikings on Constantinople, the city's distance and the effort required for an attack were simply too great for raiding to be worthwhile. Instead, the Vikings and the Byzantines signed a series of treaties, in which the Rus were accepted as a class of merchants, able to apply for licenses and certificates to sell their wares in Constantinople.

Vikings in Constantinople found a new and unexpected role as mercenaries. The Byzantine Emperors placed so little trust in the factions among their own followers that they preferred to have a private army of foreign soldiers as their personal bodyguards. With their fierce reputation and complete lack of interest in imperial matters, the Vikings made ideal guardsmen. The Greeks called them Varangoi, or pledgers, for the oath they swore to serve the emperors, and the Varangian Guard was born.

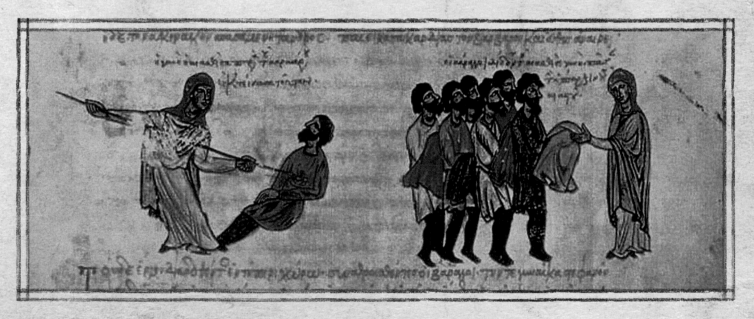

Above: Varangian guardsmen in the Skylitzis Chronicle *from the eleventh-century*

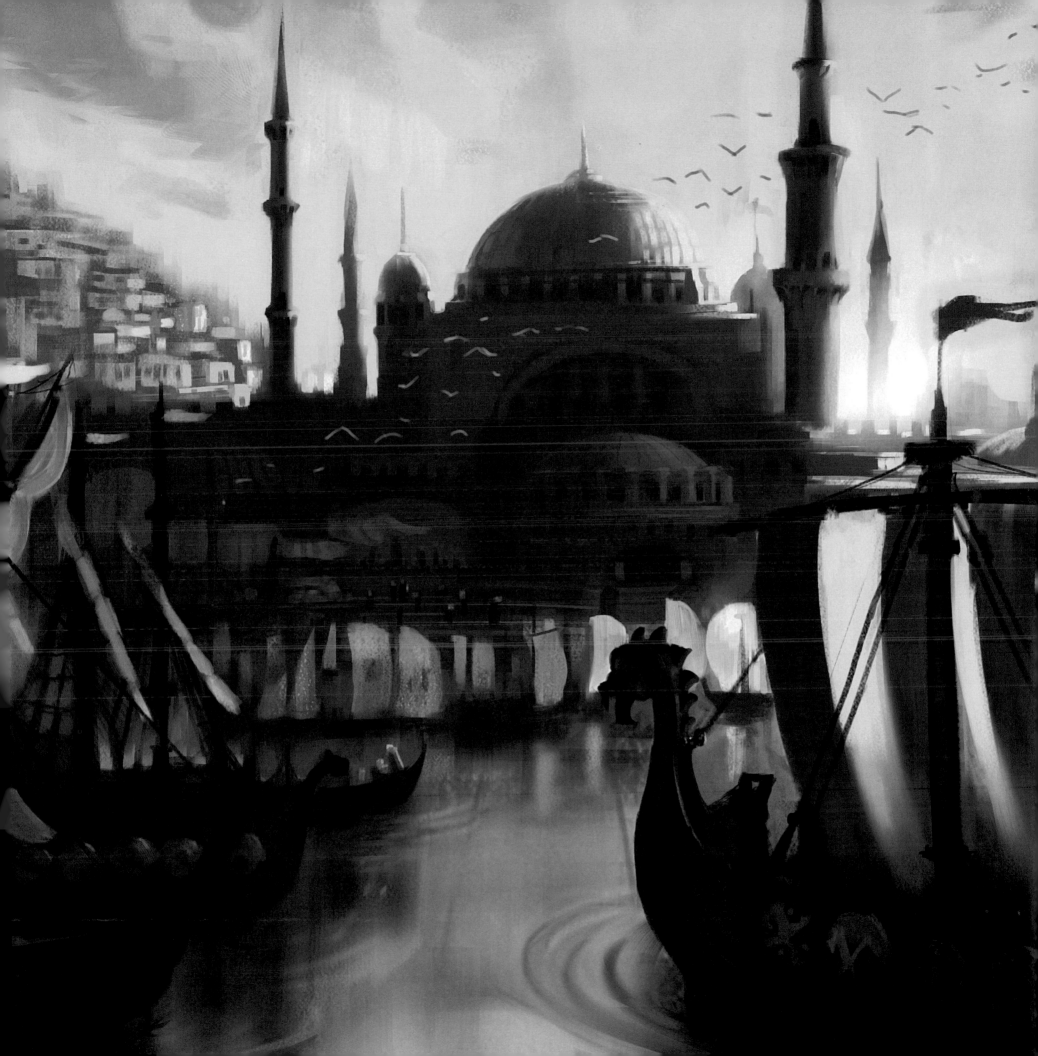

The Varangian Guard

The Varangian Guard was founded in 988 by Emperor Basil II as a special unit of Viking warriors, using recruits sent from Vladimir the Great, Rus prince of Kiev. Varangian guards were the highest paid soldiers in the Byzantine world, and they achieved superhero status in their homeland, with survivors returning to Scandinavia after many years of service, laden with gold, silks, and exotic stories. They were valued by the Byzantines because they were loyal only to money, and the Emperor was usually the richest man around. This usually ensured that they would not change sides during an attempted coup. They were, however, despised by the Byzantines for their notoriety as heavy drinkers, dangerous fighters, and uncouth attendees at religious ceremonies. Hagia Sophia, the largest cathedral in medieval Constantinople, still bears the faint remains of a piece of Viking graffiti—the name Halfdan, scratched into the marble of a balcony by an otherwise forgotten Varangian.

Varangian guardsmen fought all over the Byzantine Empire in its wars against Muslims in Sicily, what is now Turkey, and the Holy Land. Their most famous member was Harald the Ruthless, a future king of Norway, who joined under an assumed name to make his fortune before leaving Constantinople to regain his birthright.

90

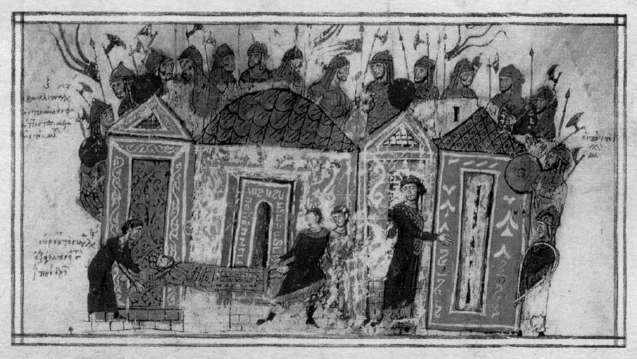

Above: Varangian guardsmen illustration from the eleventh-century Skylitzis Chronicle

THE DISCOVERY OF ICELAND

Icelandic legend tells that the island was first settled by free Norwegians who fled the imposition of kingly rule on their homeland by Harald Fairhair. Although that may have been true for some settlers, many arrived long before Harald's rise to power.

The Early Arrivals

Iceland was probably not discovered by Vikings at all, but by Irish monks, some of whom made daring pilgrimages out into the open sea, intending to live as hermits wherever their boats made landfall. However, these hermits were soon scared off by the arrival of tougher visitors.

The island was first called Gardarsholm, after Gardar the Swede, the Norse mariner who accidentally landed there when blown off course in the North Atlantic around A.D. 860. Gardar sailed around the island and spent the winter there, before returning to his family in the Hebrides. The next visitor to arrive was Naddod, a sailor from the Faeroe Islands, whose crewmembers were distinctly unimpressed with what they saw, and named the place Snowland. The island was next located by Raven-Floki, a sailor intent on settling, who followed the path of birds released from his ship, and briefly settled there. Raven-Floki was taken by surprise by the severity of a local winter, and conferred the name of Iceland on the failed colony as he slunk back home.

The first true colonists arrived via Ireland. Approximately 400 settlers arrived, mainly of Norse stock, although about fifty Irish slaves accompanied them. The first group, led by a man named Hjorleif immediately settled on the coast. The second group, led by a man named Ingolf, preferred to trust in the power of the gods, and threw their sacred wooden pillars of Thor over the side of their ship, swearing to settle only where the pillars washed ashore. An uprising among his slaves saw Hjorleif killed. The Irish escaped to some off-shore islands, where they were eventually hunted down and killed by a vengeful Ingolf. Ingolf's pillars did not properly wash ashore for another two years, after which he founded the first permanent settlement in Iceland.

91

Much of Iceland is uninhabitable and the best land was taken by 930. Although the Icelanders were supposedly peaceful settlers, their frontier was a lawless one, rife with vendettas and feuds. Loose control was imposed in the tenth century at "things"—regular council meetings where grievances were aired and the laws were recited from memory by an elected headman, or Lawspeaker.

92

Outlawry

Some form of control was maintained through "outlawry." If a jury found a man guilty of a crime, he could be pronounced an outlaw, which would result in the confiscation of his property and the disinheritance of his children. Far from solving the problem, the sentence often exported it, since many such outlaws sought new fortunes as Vikings and mercenaries back in Europe. It was illegal for any Icelander to give an outlaw food or shelter, and outlaws could be killed without fear of reprisal. "Lesser" outlawry, if the criminal paid a ransom or damages, could be limited to a three-year period, after which the convict was permitted to return to Icelandic society.

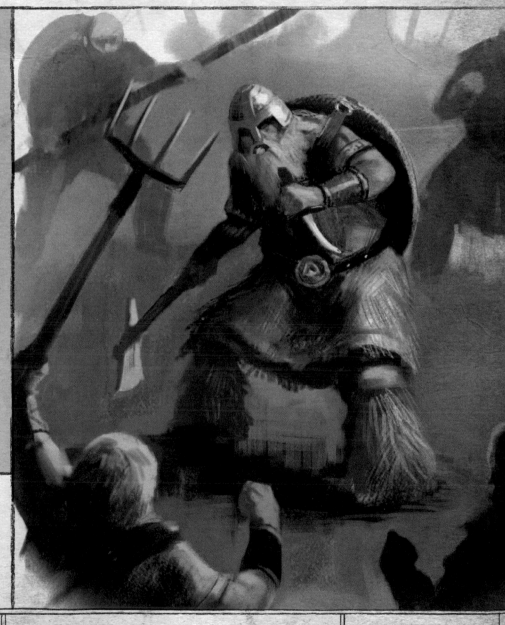

FROM PAGANS TO CHRISTIANS

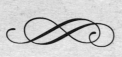 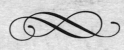

Although the descendants of the Vikings claimed to be Christians by the late Middle Ages, the progress of their conversion and their casting aside of their old gods was long, and often violent.

The first inroads made by Christians into Scandinavia were reported in Widukind's *Saxon Chronicle* around 970, in which he mentioned that a priest named Poppo impressed King Harald Bluetooth with the "power of the Christian god" by successfully lifting a red hot poker out of a fire without incurring permanent damage to his hand. Some variants of the story claim that Poppo was completely unharmed, although others explicitly mention the time his hand took to heal after the injuries he sustained.

The story, however, has its problems. "Poppo" sounds suspiciously like the generic term for any priest at the time, and later authorities such as Adam of Bremen suggested that Harald's "conversion" probably owed more to pressure from the German empire to the south.

By claiming to convert to Christianity, Harald would have avoided an invasion from German crusaders, associating his small young kingdom with their large, sophisticated empire to the south. Conversion also gave him an excuse to wage war on the pagan Norwegians to the north, without having to protect his southern borders against his new-found German brothers in Christ. Harald "made the Danes Christian" by converting himself—his subjects' conversion in his footsteps was implied, but certainly not the case in reality.

Christian conversion was often a waiting game. Several Popes recorded scandalous, non-Christian behavior of supposed converts, particularly in Scandinavia and Viking-occupied England. But because one generation was not entirely devout, it did not mean that their children would not be.

93

Hakon the Good

Another Harald, Harald Fairhair of Norway, sent his infant son, Hakon, to England, mainly to keep him from being killed by his violent brothers. With the Christian king Athelstan as his foster father, Hakon grew up with Christianity as a fact of life, rather than a strange foreign import.

Hakon returned to his native Norway as a king with English support, accompanied by English missionaries. But his attempts to win over the locals to his religion met with little success. In Trondheim, he was forced to take part in pagan rites or else risk losing his insecure position as "king" (really an elected ruler) of the local farmers. Then he was harangued by local strongmen who regarded the imposition of Christianity as a form of servitude. Nor were the farmers happy about the idea of days of fasting, or a Sabbath on which nobody would be permitted to work. When Hakon died, his well-intentioned followers buried him with rites to Odin, not realizing that such a concept was anathema to a true Christian.

Conversion by Majority Vote

94

The most impressive Christian conversion came in Iceland, where a missionary named Thangbrand enjoyed very little initial success. Sent by Olaf Crowbone to bring the Icelanders to heel, Thangbrand was a burly Saxon who dealt with the local inhabitants in the same way that Crowbone had been dealing with the Norwegians. A local sorcerer refused to obey Thangbrand, and was cut down for his defiance, as was the skald Veturlidi, who composed a song ridiculing Thangbrand's efforts, and got an ax in his skull by way of return.

Shipwrecked, outcast, and ridiculed for his efforts, Thangbrand eventually returned to Norway to report his failure, whereupon Crowbone found a new way to encourage the Icelanders to accept Jesus. He cut off the Icelanders' lifeline to Europe, refusing to send any ships from Norway, the sole source of trade with the remote colony, and refusing to allow any ships crewed by "heathens" to dock in his own country.

The news created an impossible situation back in Iceland. Local pagans were insulted by the implication that they were being held ransom over their religious beliefs, and Iceland seemed ready to split along sectarian lines. The situation was resolved by the long-serving Lawspeaker of Iceland, Thorgeir Thorkelsson, who found a delicate way to bring the two parties together before they came to blows.

Hakon's Good Intentions

An extract from the saga of Hakon the Good by Snorri Sturluson
(in which Hakon tries the gentle approach)

King Hakon was a good Christian when he came to Norway; but as the whole country was heathen... he resolved to practice his Christianity in private. But he kept Sundays, and the Friday fasts, and some token of the greatest holy days. He made a law that the festival of Yule should begin at the same time as Christian people held it..."

Under his rule, the beginning of Yule, or the slaughter night, was the night of mid-winter (14th December), and Yule was kept for three days thereafter. It was his intent, as soon as he had set himself fast in the land, and had subjected the whole to his power, to introduce Christianity. He went to work first by enticing to Christianity the men who were dearest to him; and many, out of friendship to him, allowed themselves to be baptized, and some laid aside sacrifices. He dwelt long in the Trondheim district, for the strength of the country lay there; and when he thought that, by the support of some powerful people there, he could set up Christianity he sent a message to England for a bishop and other teachers; and when they arrived in Norway, Hakon made it known that he would proclaim Christianity over all the land.

96

Conversion Confusions

An extract from the saga of Hakon the Good by Snorri Sturluson
(in which Hakon faces strong resistance, and eventually resorts to brute force)

The winter thereafter the king prepared a Yule feast... [But local lords swore] to root out Christianity in Norway, and four others swore that they would force King Hakon to offer sacrifice to the old gods. Four first went in four ships southwards to More, and killed three priests, and burnt three churches, and then they returned.

JELLING CHURCHYARD

Jelling is a small town on the Jutland peninsula that was the home of Gorm III (also known as Gorm the Old), whose son, Harald Bluetooth, would unify all of Denmark. Both Gorm and his wife were buried in a pagan fashion, in large burial mounds. When Harald converted to Christianity, he built a church at the sacred pagan site, perhaps hoping to convert his parents to Christianity even beyond the grave.

A smaller, older stone erected by Harald's father, Gorm, celebrates the memory of Harald's mother, Thyra, legendarily (and somewhat doubtfully) said to have been a daughter of the English king Aethelred, calling her the "Glory of Denmark." Some legends suggest that Thyra was also a Christian, and that even if she were buried in a pagan manner, her son built the church nearby in an attempt to Christianize the burial site, and hence his mother's fate in the afterlife.

But Jelling is most famous for the larger stone that towers above the first. The larger stone dates from Harald Bluetooth's reign, and honors his parents' memory while pointing firmly to the Christianizing of Denmark.

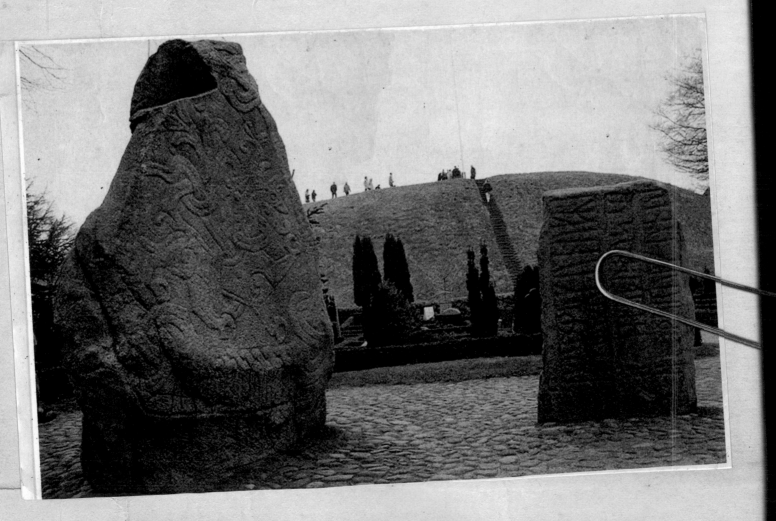

THE JELLING STONE

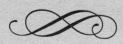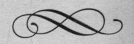

The larger Jelling Stone marks the point where Christianity achieved prominence in Denmark. It is a slab of memorial rock like so many thousands of rune stones around Scandinavia, but its letters do not speak of pagan rites or imagery. Instead, it serves, in a modern sense, as a headstone for the graves of two parents, and an announcement of a powerful and influential religious conversion.

But the forgotten star of the Jelling carvings is the woman who is mentioned in them twice—a lady of legendary religious virtue and mythical beauty, whose virtue supposedly shamed her husband into tolerating (if not accepting) Christian beliefs, and whose strength of will became an example in Danish legend. But Harald Bluetooth was the younger son of Gorm and Thyra. His elder brother Knut died in a foreign battle, which legends claimed had been foretold on Gorm's wedding night. The story of Thyra's marriage, her husband's dream, and the fulfillment of the prophecy in Gorm's old age, were repeated in the History of the Danes, by Saxo Grammaticus.

TRANSLITERATION

(side A) *haraltr : kunukR : baþ : kaurua kubl : þausi : aft : kurm faþur sinauk aft : þąurui : muþur : sina : saharaltr (:) ias : sąR * uan * tanmaurk* (side B) ala * auk * nuruiak (side C) * auk * t(a)ni (* karþi *) kristną*

TRANSLATION

"King Harald ordered this monument made in memory of Gorm, his father, and in memory of Thyra, his mother; that Harald who won for himself all of Denmark and Norway and made the Danes Christian."

INTERPRETATION

The proclamation on the Jelling Stone is sometimes known as the "Baptism of Denmark," since Harald's bold claim is that of a lord who expects all of his subjects to follow his religious beliefs. In the past, this might have meant the veneration of a particular Norse god—Odin perhaps, or Thor. But Harald's claim that he had "made the Danes Christian" was a critical moment in the history of the spread of missionaries through the north. Christianity was no longer a cult on the periphery; it was the preferred religion of the most powerful man in the region.

Sword and Cross

At the turn of the millennium some voyages, such as those to Greenland and Vinland, may have been encouraged, at least in part, by some pagans' desire to flee the growing power of Christianity in Iceland.

In the year 1000, the Icelandic Thing council reached a complex compromise. The entire country would accept Christianity in order to appease the distant Norwegians. The old pagan ways were criminalized, although a handy loophole permitted devout worshippers of the old gods to continue their rituals in private. Technically, this too was illegal, but since nobody would see the pagan rituals unless invited into an Icelander's home, pagans were allowed to continue in their own fashion.

Thorgeir guaranteed the Icelanders that they were still free to leave disabled children out in the cold to die, and that they could still eat horse meat—an unknown reference to a religious ceremony, possibly in honor of the god Frey. However, not even these pagan ways survived long. The official Christian status of Iceland was largely internalized by the next generation, and, despite Thorgeir's promise, such pagan practices were also outlawed.

95

Tough Love

It was the two Olafs—Olaf "Crowbone" Tryggvason and Olaf the Stout—who eventually brought Christianity to Norway with any degree of permanence. They did so by offering locals a clear choice: accept the love of Christ or be put to the sword. Crowbone ordered pagan "sorcerers" to be tied to rocks at low tide, where they were left to drown.

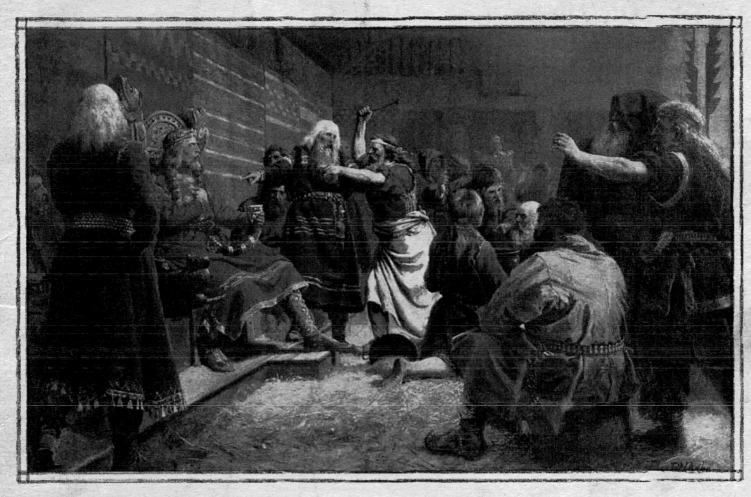

Above: Hakon the Good *by P.N. Arbo*

Now, when King Hakon came, the freemen assembled in great numbers; and immediately, on the first day of the feast, insisted hard that he should offer sacrifice, and threatened him with violence if he refused. Earl Sigurd tried to make peace between them, and brought it so far that the king took some bits of horse-liver, and emptied all the goblets the freemen filled for him without the sign of the cross; but as soon as the feast was over, the king and the earl went home. The king was very angry... saying that the next time he came to Trondheim, he would come with such strength of men-at-arms that he would repay the freemen for their behavior.

THE TROUBLE WITH CONVERSION

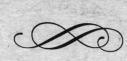

Although there were many attempts to convert the Vikings to Christianity, it was a slow process. Peaceful farmers and fishermen might be persuaded to choose Christianity, but Viking warriors clung to their battle-religion and their old gods.

The experience of Viking traders in the Christian world persuaded many that Christianity was worth considering. Saint Olga, a Rus queen, reputedly fell to her knees in awe at the sight of the Hagia Sophia cathedral in Constantinople. She converted to Christianity, and although her son did not, her grandson Saint Vladimir did. Many Christian missionaries were happy to play a waiting game.

Viking settlers in England grew up with churches in their midst, and even if they paid no heed to the "new" religion, often their wives or their children did. Some leaders accepted Christianity as a condition for signing deals or treaties with kingdoms. Olga's grandson Saint Vladimir, for example, eventually married Anna, a daughter of the Byzantine emperor, ensuring that the church in what would become Russia was tied to the Eastern Orthodox rite of Constantinople, and not the Catholic Christianity of Western Europe at the time.

The new religion also provided Vikings with a new excuse for conflict, as Christian converts waged holy war on their pagan cousins, hoping to save their souls, possibly while stealing their treasure. However, Christianity did not always unite different races in brotherhood.

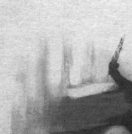

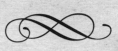

98

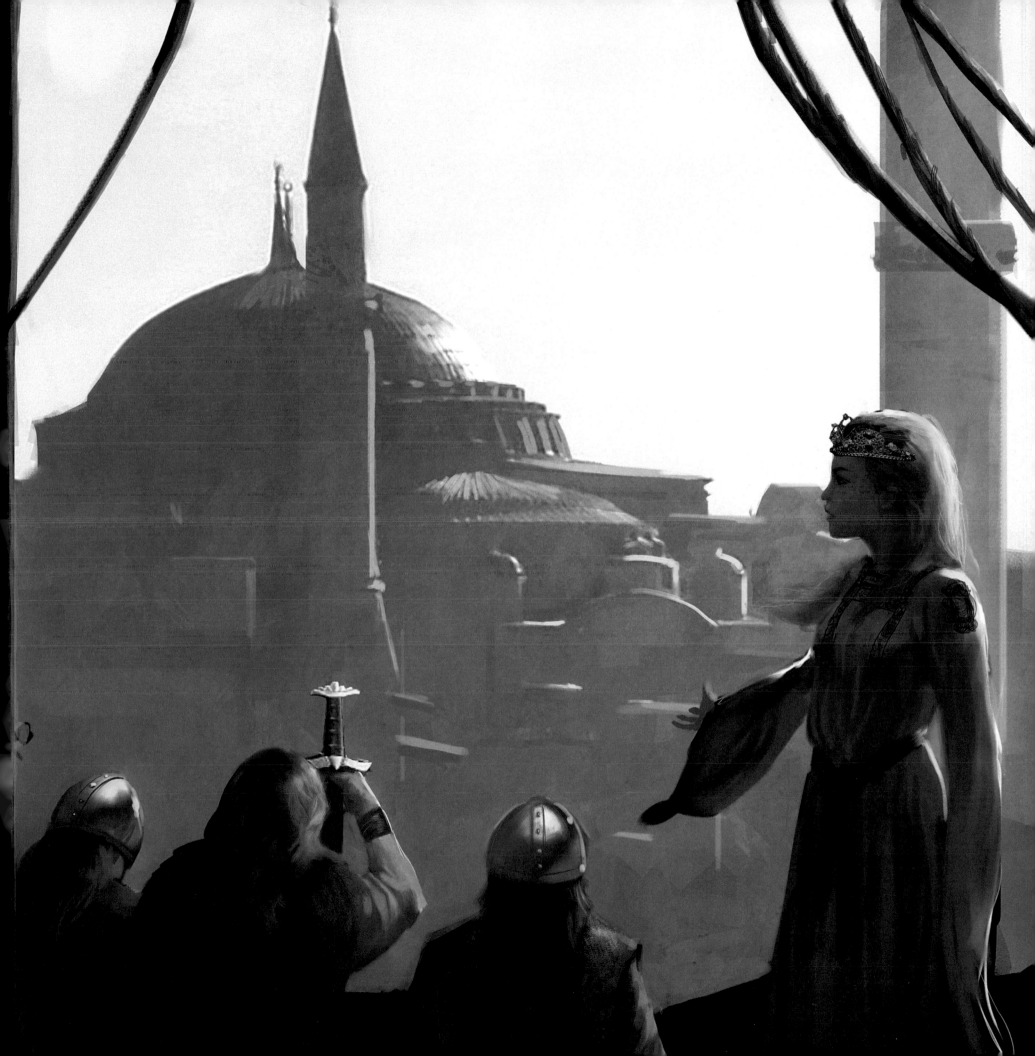

The Danelaw

The Vikings who settled in England were nominally Christian, although church leaders registered complaints that many of them were continuing pagan religious sacrifices. Ever since Alfred's treaty with Guthrum, the descendants of the Vikings enjoyed their own laws and customs, supposedly without interference, and the north and much of the east of England was known as the "Danelaw"—a place where Scandinavian law held sway. In particular, disputes in the Danelaw could be settled through trial by combat—a typical way Vikings dealt with problems. Evidence from place-names demonstrates that the descendants of Vikings were still very much in the minority and surrounded by Anglo-Saxon locals.

St. Brice's Day

We can only guess the tensions that led to the St. Brice's Day Massacre on November 13, 1002, when King Aethelred II of England ordered the deaths of all the Scandinavians in England, accusing them of wanting to "ensnare his life." In Oxford, the local immigrant population fled to a local church and barricaded themselves inside, hoping that the holy ground would give them some form of protection. Instead, they were locked inside and burned alive.

100

Aethelred the "Unready"

King Aethelred II of England (966-1016) became king at a very young age after the murder of his half-brother Edward. His advisors took control at a time when England was plagued by invaders, leading to his nickname "Aethelred the Unready." The name derives from the English belief that he was lacking good counsel, or rede, and is perhaps best translated as Aethelred the Ill-Advised. Aethelred attempted to find new allies by marrying Emma of Normandy, herself a descendant of Vikings.

Whether there was a Viking conspiracy against Aethelred or not, retribution soon arrived. The Viking leader Svein Forkbeard, who had already raided England on several occasions, now returned with an invasion fleet, claiming that his sister had been one of the people killed on St. Brice's Day.

A decree was sent out by me with the counsel of my leading men and magnates, to the effect that all the Danes who had sprung up in this island, sprouting like weeds among the wheat, were to be destroyed by a most just extermination.

—Aethelred II

101

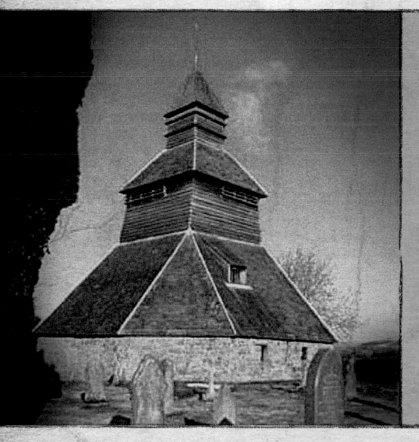

Daneskin

A modern reminder of the hatred in the Danelaw of the English toward Vikings can be found in several English churches, whose doors, as legend has it, were covered with the skins of Viking prisoners. Although many of these coverings proved to be mere cow leather, local legend often claimed that the church doors had been covered with "Daneskin" flayed from the bodies of captured Viking invaders.

Above: St Mary the Virgin's Church in Pembridge, England

Life In The Danelaw

Place-names throughout eastern England show the former presence of a small but influential population of Scandinavians, ruling over the local inhabitants. The unit of administration in the Danelaw revolved around "hundreds," a hundred being the area of land sufficient to support a hundred peasant families. A hundred was also known as a Wapentake (Norse: *vapnatak*), the reference being to the recruitment of warriors (a weapon-take), or to the sound of the clashing of swords on shields, which would be a significant feature of Norse-style council meetings.

As might be expected, laws in the Danelaw were different from Saxon England. There were much heavier fines for breaching the peace (i.e., disobeying the orders of one's lord), and it was common for many legal cases to be settled through trial by combat. Residents of the Danelaw, as relatively recent arrivals, without debts or obligations, who had seized their land from previous owners, were also far more likely to be free men rather than indentured serfs. Many decades later, at the time of the Norman conquest and the ensuing Doomsday Book survey of England, the number of free landholders in the old Danelaw was still noticeable, although by this time many of them were struggling as farmers; most would subsequently lose their free status by falling into debt to local potentates, in effect becoming just like the average Anglo-Saxon.

102

Clement Of The Danes

Those Scandinavians who spent the most time in the Christian west were most likely to become Christians themselves. Their first choice of patron saint seems to have reflected contemporary fashions, but also their interest in the sea.

Saint Clement was the fourth pope of the Christian faith, exiled to a distant stone quarry by the Emperor Trajan. There, he irritated his captors by discovering a spring to quench his fellow prisoners' thirst, and he was eventually drowned by imperial order, thrown into the Black Sea tied to an anchor. His watery death led to his eventual recognition as a patron saint of mariners, and many areas of Scandinavian settlement gained a church dedicated to "Saint Clement of the Danes." Clement was also a patron saint of blacksmiths, and appears in Saxon folktales dating from the time of King Alfred, in which he supposedly offered magical aid to Alfred's own craftsmen.

SVEIN FORKBEARD AND CANUTE THE GREAT

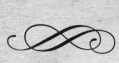 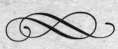

Despite his claim that he was avenging the death of his sister (who may not have even existed), Svein Forkbeard probably had another reason for his attack on England. When Forkbeard was not leading ships against them, the English were being attacked by other Vikings. One, Thorkell the Tall, had amassed so much money in bribes and Danegeld that Forkbeard was afraid of how he might spend that money back in Scandinavia—perhaps by making a bid for the throne of Denmark. Instead, Svein attacked Thorkell in England, pre-empting a conflict in Scandinavia by fighting the battle in a distant land.

The Death of Aelfheah

Over the years, Vikings had learned that a sure way to make fast cash was to kidnap a prominent person and hold them for ransom. A party of raiders in 1011 managed to capture Aelfheah (Saint Alfege), the archbishop of Canterbury, in Kent. They demanded 3,000 lbs. of silver for his release, but the priest refused. Aelfheah had been an active missionary among Vikings and had previously managed to secure the conversions of several prominent leaders, including Olaf "Crowbone" Tryggvason. However, his luck had run out. His captors grew increasingly annoyed with his refusal to either pay them ransom or allow one of his associates to come up with the money. Eventually, he was murdered during a drunken banquet. He managed to achieve something in death, however. The Viking leader Thorkell the Tall was said to disapprove of the manner of Aelfheah's demise, which may have been a factor in encouraging his own decision to turn on the Vikings and fight on behalf of his former English enemies.

103

Thorkell the Tall switched sides, but even with his assistance, the English were unable to hold off Svein's army, which swelled with new recruits from the Danelaw, who felt closer to the Scandinavian invaders than to the English who had recently tried to kill them all on St. Brice's Day. Within the year, King Aethelred II had fled to his second wife's homeland in Normandy, and Svein was ready to proclaim himself king of England. However, he did not have long to enjoy his victory, and he died of illness before he could be crowned. Aethelred returned to the kingdom, but was soon embroiled in a second war against Svein's son Canute (Knut).

London Bridge is Falling Down

During the fighting between the sons of Aethelred and Svein, a Viking fleet sailed up the River Thames and established a base on the south bank, known as the Suthvirke or "South Fort"—in the area now called Southwark. The English had fortified London Bridge in the manner of the earlier French defenses at places such as Pont de l'Arche. One brave Viking mercenary, Olaf the Stout, sailed right up to the bridge amid a hail of missiles, and attached ropes to it. His men then rowed downstream with all their might, pulling down the already-damaged bridge, and leading to the famous nursery rhyme "London Bridge is Falling Down." Olaf (later Saint Olaf) still gives his name to a couple of streets in the Southwark area: St. Olaf's Stairs and Tooley Street (i.e.,'T Olaf Street).

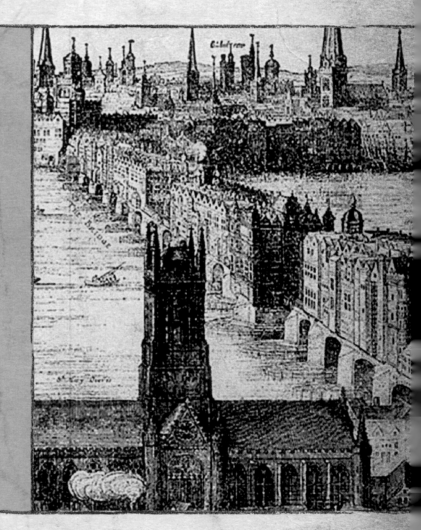

Above: London Bridge in 1616

Canute the Great

Canute was chosen as Svein's successor by the army, but was forced to leave temporarily when Aethelred returned. Coming back with another army in 1015, he fought against Aethelred's son Edmund Ironside, and became the king of England upon his enemy's death in 1016. He married Aethelred's widow, Emma of Normandy, and soon became the ruler of a loose empire of the North Sea—he was also elected king of Denmark in 1019 after the death of his own brother, and in 1028 he overthrew Olaf the Stout to become the overlord of Norway. He gained the kingship of Sweden in 1030. However, his empire did not survive long after his death that same year. His sons were given separate portions to rule, and they soon fought among themselves and with other claimants.

Ruling the Waves

The most famous legend of Canute is the story of his attempt to command the sea itself. He supposedly did so in an attempt to silence the constant flattery of his courtiers, who persisted in telling him that he was truly great. When, as expected, he failed to make the tide turn, he supposedly refused to ever wear his crown again, and claimed that the only true king was Jesus. However, the entire story is likely to be a fabrication by Canute's supporters.

Sanding the Streets

A strange custom persists in the English town of Knutsford ("Canute's-crossing"), where the king was said to have wished a newlywed couple as many children as the grains of sand he threw from his shoes. To this day, local inhabitants celebrate this by making sand-pictures on the streets each May Day. However, Canute may have never even visited Knutsford—even if it does get its name from a Scandinavian visitor, there is no evidence that the Knut of Knutsford was "Canute the Great."

OLAF THE STOUT

Olaf the Stout (c.995–1030) was a minor descendant of Harald Fairhair, the first king of Norway. He grew up in south Norway and left as a teenager to become a mercenary, fighting for Thorkell the Tall during Svein's invasion, before switching sides and becoming a mercenary working for King Aethelred the Unready.

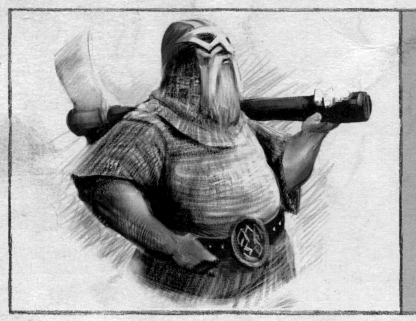

"That Fat Man"

Olaf seems to have been shorter and stockier than the average Viking, and was described by his own father-in-law as "that fat man." He is often depicted holding an ax—a weapon he preferred over the more aristocratic sword favored by most other Viking leaders.

106

When the victory of Canute removed the need for mercenaries, Olaf returned to his Viking ways, making a couple of raids along the coast of England before returning to Norway. Annoyed at being ruled by an absentee monarch and swayed by family connections, many Norwegians hailed Olaf, not Canute, as their rightful king. He also married one of the daughters of the king of Sweden, establishing himself with Scandinavian connections to rival those of Canute. With Canute's supporters in control of the English coasts, Olaf spent the 1020s with his attention on local matters, except for a mission into Finland to collect tribute during which his men found the locals violently unwelcoming.

Canute eventually sent envoys demanding that Olaf recognize him as his overlord—he was happy to leave Olaf in charge of Norway, but would require him to pay a tribute of his own in the form of regular bribes. Olaf refused, but he was already losing support in Norway. Canute won over numerous groups with gifts and promises, so that when his forces arrived in 1028, Olaf was forced to flee into exile among the Rus.

However, Olaf was not gone for long. Canute left his own infant son in charge in Norway, with the boy's English mother, Aelfgifu, as regent. Aelfgifu, sent from Northampton to Norway to allow Canute to marry Emma for political reasons, was deeply unpopular with the Norwegians, who soon seemed ready to welcome Olaf back as their ruler.

In 1030, Olaf the Stout returned to Scandinavia with almost 500 men, mainly Rus and fellow exiles, whose ranks were soon swelled by Swedish fortune-seekers. By the time he went into battle at Stiklastad near Trondheim, his forces totaled just under 4,000. They faced an army of some 14,000 defenders, and the vastly outnumbered Olaf was killed in the struggle. Since Olaf's attempted reconquest of Norway was framed by local skalds as a conflict between a Christian nobleman and local pagans, his death in battle was regarded as a form of Christian martyrdom, and he became the object of a local Christian cult, centered on his burial site at the Nitharos cathedral.

107

Saint Olaf

Olaf was soon made a saint, after rumors spread of ghostly appearances and the magical healing powers of his blood. Several bad harvests after his death, thought to be caused by the angry Christian God, sealed his reputation as a Christian ruler who had been martyred. He is now the patron saint of Norway.

Above: A representation of Saint Olaf at Overselo Church in Sweden

HARALD THE RUTHLESS

Olaf's half-brother, Harald the Ruthless, was only a teenage boy at the time of the Battle of Stiklastad. He was forced to flee the battlefield and sought refuge first in Sweden, then across the Baltic Sea among the Rus Vikings in what is now Russia.

With no money or prospects, Harald found work doing what Vikings did best—fighting. He served the Rus for three years as a mercenary in local vendettas, before deciding that richer rewards awaited him to the south in Constantinople. Joining the Varangian Guard under an assumed name, he fought in numerous Byzantine wars, and may have also served as a guardsman on a rare imperial pilgrimage to the Holy Land, where he bathed in the Jordan River.

Returning to Scandinavia many years later as a rich and successful warrior with a Rus princess for his bride, Harald bullied his nephew, Magnus the Good, into giving him half of his lands, which spread across Denmark and Norway. He soon found himself fighting the Danish lord Svein Estrithson in a protracted war over who had the right to rule the region. Eventually, in 1064, the two rival Vikings fought each other to a draw, and recognized each other's right to rule. Now in his fifties, Harald the Ruthless decided on a new target, and determined to invade England.

108

Hard Ruler

Harald got his nickname from his fierce reputation for showing no mercy. A life spent on the run and in military service under unpredictable masters had turned him into a no-nonsense warrior who was called Hardraada—"Hard-Ruler," "Severe in Counsel," or just plain "Ruthless."

with no money, Harald found work doing what Vikings did best—fighting

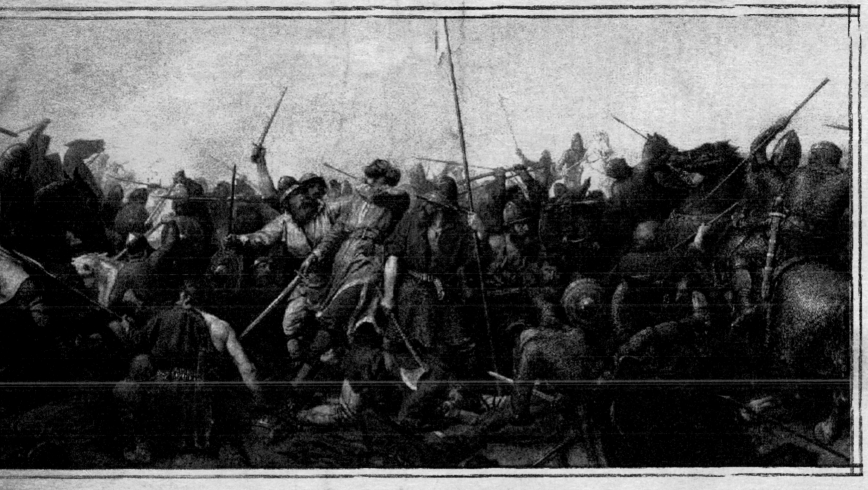

Above: Battle of Stamford Bridge *by P.N. Arbo*

Claiming that he was the rightful heir of Canute the Great, Harald arrived in north England with a fleet of ships. He swiftly conquered the old Viking enclave of York, but was defeated by English defenders at the Battle of Stamford Bridge in 1066. The English had speed-marched all the way from the south, but still inflicted a crushing defeat on the Vikings, who fled with only twenty-four ships out of their original 300.

Harald fell in battle at Stamford Bridge, which is widely regarded as the last major battle against Vikings to be fought on English soil. Although his death was a major event in the history of the Viking era, it is usually over-shadowed by a much more famous event occurring only days later.

THE NORMAN CONQUEST

Even as the survivors of the Norwegian invasion limped home after defeating Harald the Ruthless in the north of England, the Anglo-Saxon defenders had to march south to deal with a second invasion. Weeks later, the English were forced to accept a new king, William the Conqueror, and the age of the Anglo-Saxons was over.

History does not record the Norman Conquest as a Viking victory, yet the Normans were the descendants of those same raiders who had plagued the north coast of France in the ninth century. The Viking leader Hrolf the Walker signed a deal with the Frankish king Charles the Simple, wherein he would receive land on the north coast of France if he promised to keep other Viking raiders from sailing up the Seine River. A century later, the descendants of Hrolf the "North Man" were the Dukes of "Normandy." As in other places, the original Viking inhabitants were in a minority, and many of their children took French names or spouses. The Normans did not trade with their relatives back home either—there are relatively few Norman coins to be found in Scandinavian archaeological sites. Despite their swift adoption of a Frankish lifestyle, the Normans maintained some ties to their Scandinavian cousins. The Danish language was spoken in the ducal family for several generations, and the Normans received numerous complaints from the English across the channel who believed, rightly, that Norman ports were serving as bases for some of the "Scandinavian" raiders who continued to attack England.

William the Conqueror

Duke William of Normandy had expected the childless King Edward the Confessor of England to nominate him as his successor. Instead, upon Edward's death, the English chose Harold Godwinson as their new ruler, prompting William to invade. William's invasion, however, displays little sign of Viking trademarks. He used his ships only for a brief crossing of the channel, fighting the majority of his battles on foot or horseback. He did, however, benefit from the exhaustion of the English defenders caused by the earlier conflict with Harald the Ruthless. William famously defeated the English at the Battle of Hastings in 1066, but still had to contend with Viking raids.

The Harrowing of the North

Viking descendants in the north of England held out against the Norman invaders, and called upon the assistance of Svein Estrithson, who had inherited the claim on the English throne previously held by Harald the Ruthless. In 1069, a fleet of 240 Scandinavian ships, led by Svein's son, successfully captured York. The Normans responded with the "harrowing of the north," a terrifying campaign of mayhem, burning, and destruction, designed to both punish the rebellious north and to make it an unattractive destination for future Vikings.

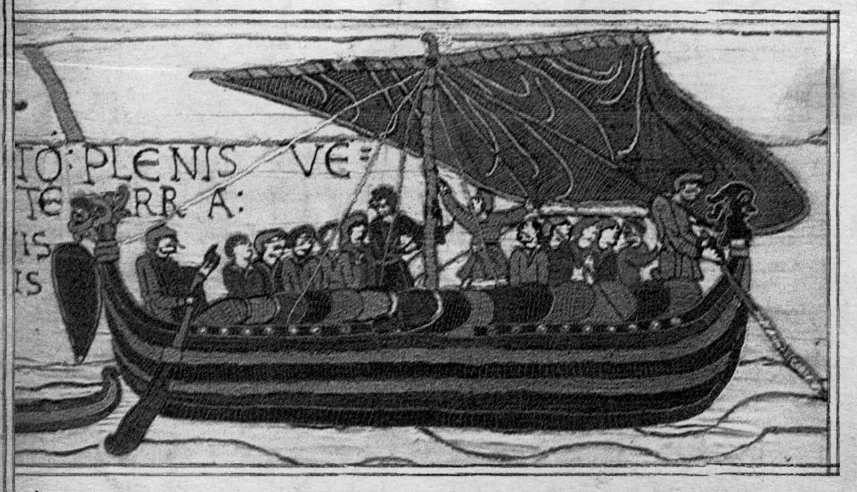

Above: Bayeux tapestry

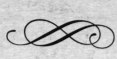 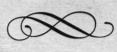

ERIK THE RED AND GREENLAND

While some descendants of the Vikings fought over the kingdoms of Europe, some distant outposts discovered completely new lands.

Although Icelanders were farmers and fishermen, a Viking element persisted in their society. Erik, son of Torvald, was a Norwegian exile whose family had fled their homeland after his father was accused of manslaughter. Erik gained the nickname Erik the Red, either from the color of his hair or from the fiery nature of his temper, which he had inherited from his father. As an adult, Erik proved to be his father's son when he quarreled with his neighbors leading to further deaths. Exiled from Iceland for several years under a sentence of lesser outlawry, he chose to sail west, in search of a new land to settle. Erik's home in western Iceland was close to a local mountain peak, from which, on a good day, the hillingar mirage effect made it possible to see what might be more land on the horizon.

112

If Erik was searching for land further west, he must have been truly desperate to get away from Iceland, as there was little evidence at the time that he might find anything worthwhile. Greenland is the largest island in the world, although most of it is covered by glaciers. It was first seen by the Norse sailor Gunnbjorn Ulf-Krakson in the early tenth century, when he was blown off course and noticed a bleak, icy coastline. Fifty years later, a group led by Snaebjorn Galti tried to settle on the cluster of rocky islands off the coast of Greenland, which they called Gunnbjorn's Skerries. However, the mission was a failure, and the settlers killed each other before the year was out.

Environmental Damage

All the best land in Iceland was taken, and the trees that had dotted the island were chopped down. The early Icelanders did not realize that the trees would not grow back as fast as they would have done in Scandinavia, and soon the absence of vegetation caused the topsoil to blow away. These factors combined to make the idea of searching out more land to the west an attractive prospect to the younger generation of Icelanders.

If Erik had landed on the eastern coast of Greenland, he would have found nothing but the forbidding ice that had scared away earlier explorers. Instead, pack ice and icebergs caused him to push further south, around the southernmost point of Greenland, leading him to the habitable western coast of the island. Like Iceland, there were no trees, but plenty of green pasture land suitable for grazing, leading Erik to name the place Greenland. He probably hoped that such a positive-sounding name would encourage other Icelanders to make the dangerous crossing to the new settlement.

At the end of his exile in 986, Erik returned to Iceland and gave the locals the hard sell on Greenland. He persuaded a large number of Icelanders to accompany him, and twenty-five rickety old ships left for Greenland. Only fourteen ships survived the crossing, but the people settled in two villages in their new home.

Erik settled as a farmer in his new home of Brattahlid, and became the de facto leader of the Greenland colonies. In his old age, he originally intended to accompany his son Leif "the Lucky" Erikson on a mission further west in the year 1000, but he fell from his horse shortly before the trip, gravely injuring himself. He died a few months later from an epidemic brought on a ship from Norway, and hence never saw the legendary Vinland.

113

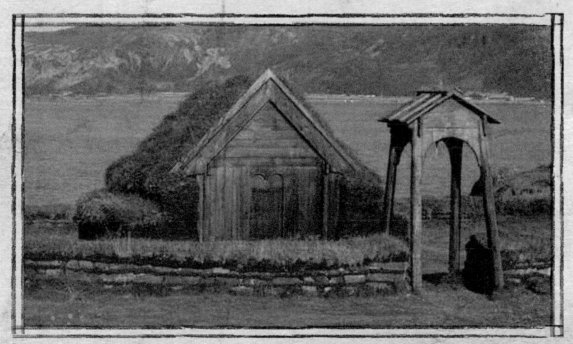

Above: A modern reproduction of Thjodhild's Church at Brattahlid, the first Church in the New World

THE DISCOVERY OF VINLAND

There was, of course, still more land to the west of Greenland. The Greenlanders had suffered from the same shortage of lumber and ships as in Iceland, and stuck to farming and herding in their new lands. Contact with their ancestral home was provided by occasional merchant ships, such as one sailed by Bjarni Herjolfsson sometime around the year 985.

Bjarni arrived in Iceland on one of his periodic visits, hoping to spend the winter at his father's farm before sailing back to Norway with a hold full of Icelandic goods to sell back home. Instead, he discovered that his father had left with the Greenland settlers. Bjarni sailed after them, but soon got lost, sailing too far to the south of Greenland. He came upon a strange shore, and sailed north along it, before realizing that Greenland must be behind him to the west. When he finally arrived at the Greenland colony, he told the settlers that he had found a place rich in forests.

114

Before long, Bjarni settled down, and fourteen years later, he sold his old boat to Erik the Red's son Leif. After listening to Bjarni's story, Leif retraced his route, sailing up the west coast of Greenland before making the relatively short crossing to what was probably Baffin Island—a flat, unimpressive location that Leif called Helluland, or "Slab Land."

Sailing south along the Canadian coast, Leif reached the forests, which he called Markland, or "Forest Land." He spent the winter in a makeshift camp now believed to have been at L'Anse aux Meadows in Newfoundland, where his fellow Vikings beached their ships, set up a smithy to make repairs, and even built a little sauna lodge. The turf huts they built, known as "Leif's Booths," would become the base for future expeditions.

he told them that he had found a place rich in forests

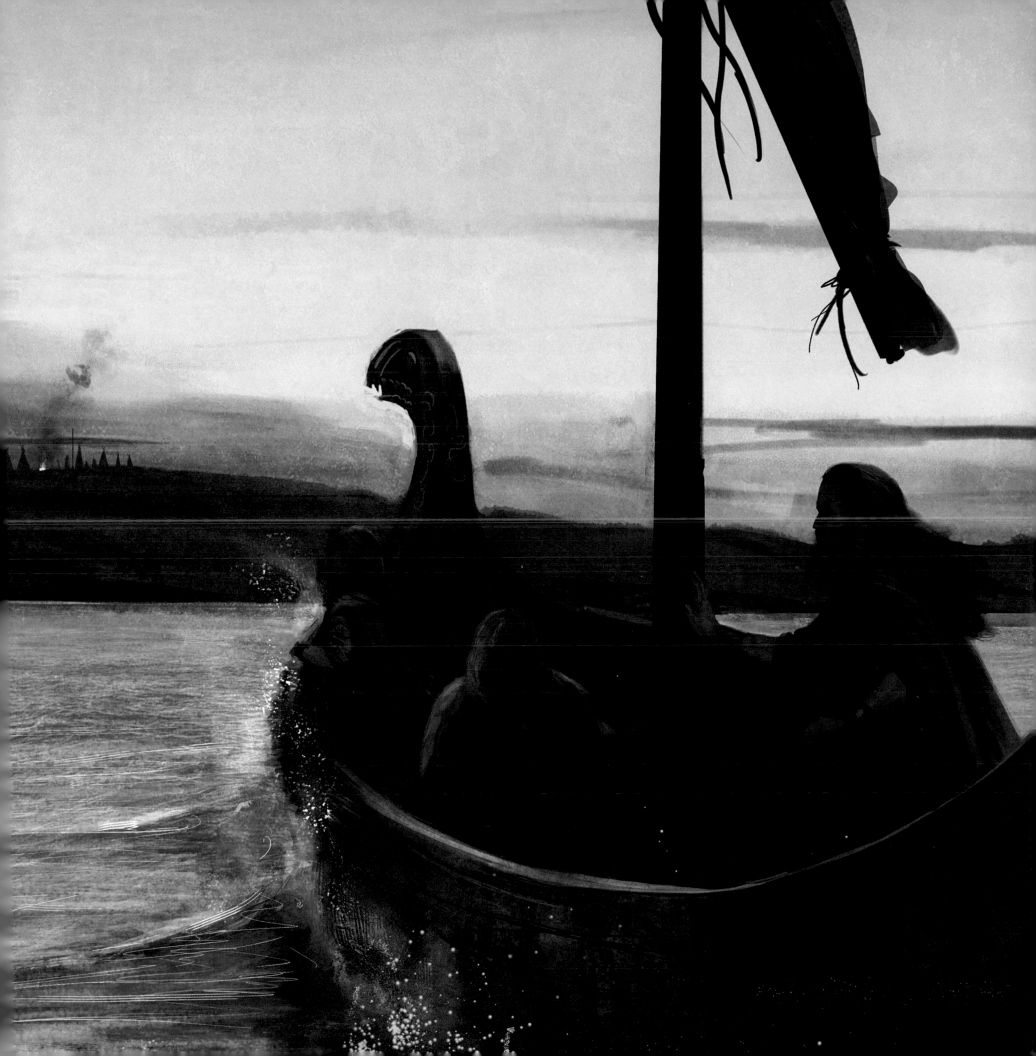

VIKINGS VERSUS SKRAELINGS

There were several further missions to Vinland by members of Leif's family. His brother Thorvald led a second expedition to the Booths, where he spent the winter before exploring further to the south. There, his men ran into people they called the Skraelings—"screechers," "flinchers," or possibly just "savages." The first recorded encounter between Europeans and Native Americans (likely to have been Beothuk or MicMac Indians), ended in a brawl, in which all but one of the Skraelings were killed. A lone survivor got away in a canoe and returned with reinforcements. Thorir was killed in the ensuing battle and many of his men lost heart.

Others, however, were encouraged by the thought of local people to trade with or perhaps even conquer. A third mission went to the Booths, led by Thorfinn Karsefni, who had recently married Leif's widowed sister-in-law Gudrid. This mission stayed long enough at the Booths for Gudrid to give birth to a son, Snorri, the first European born in America.

Initial encounters with the Skraelings were nervous but productive. The Greenlanders traded milk and red felt for furs, which the Skraelings happily brought them. Thorfinn, however, forbade his men from trading any weapons. His mistrust was justified, because lack of communication and general suspicion between the two groups soon led to another fight. Thorfinn's mission returned home with traded goods, but also with reports of fractious natives.

It was almost as far from Greenland to Leif's Booths as it was from Greenland to Norway, leading many Greenlanders to regard trips to Vinland as a waste of time. With unknown numbers of angry natives, it seemed too dangerous to all but the most foolhardy of locals.

116

it seemed too dangerous to all but the most foolhardy

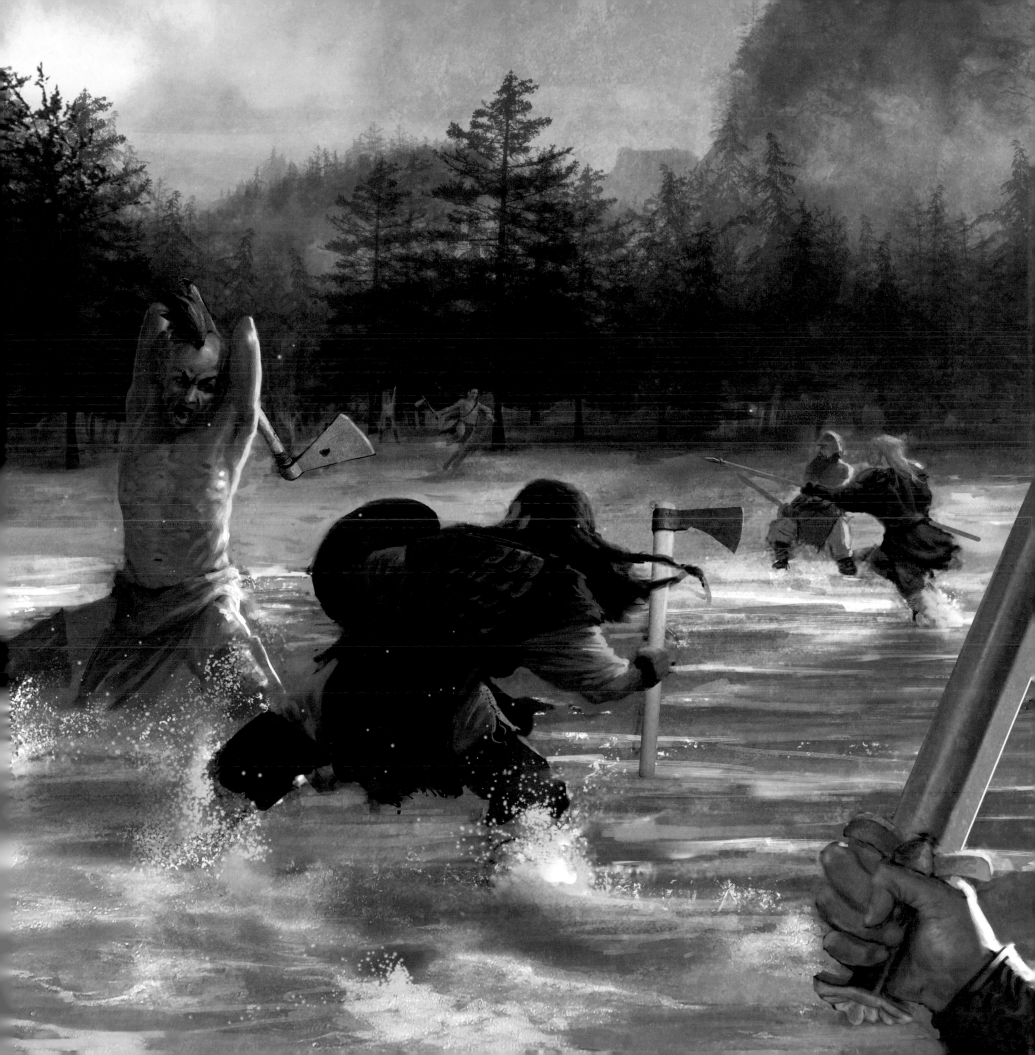

Only Leif's half-sister Freydis, a fiery woman who had inherited much of Erik's red temper, was prepared to risk another trip. She arrived with a group of settlers intending to turn the Booths into a permanent colony, but she soon quarreled with her fellow travelers. Amid further problems with the Skraelings, Freydis murdered several of her fellow colonists. The expedition returned in disgrace, and no further attempts to colonize Vinland were recorded.

As for Freydis, she tried to cover up the murders, claiming that the missing settlers had decided to stay behind. She bribed her fellow travelers to keep silent, and returned to work on her Greenland farm, hoping to forget the Vinland incident. But Leif grew suspicious, and tortured three of Freydis's men until they confessed the whole story. Upon discovering the truth, the Christian convert Leif elected not to punish her, although he did announce that he expected higher powers would cause Freydis to suffer the consequences of her crime. Thereafter, both she and her children were shunned by the Greenland community.

The Greenlanders made several more trips to Markland to pick up lumber, but appear to have stayed clear of inhabited areas ever since, until Vinland was regarded as little more than a legend. There are, however, controversial suggestions that the Freydis mission was by no means the last, and that European settlements in North America were much more permanent than historical sources suggest.

118

Vinland was regarded as little more than a legend

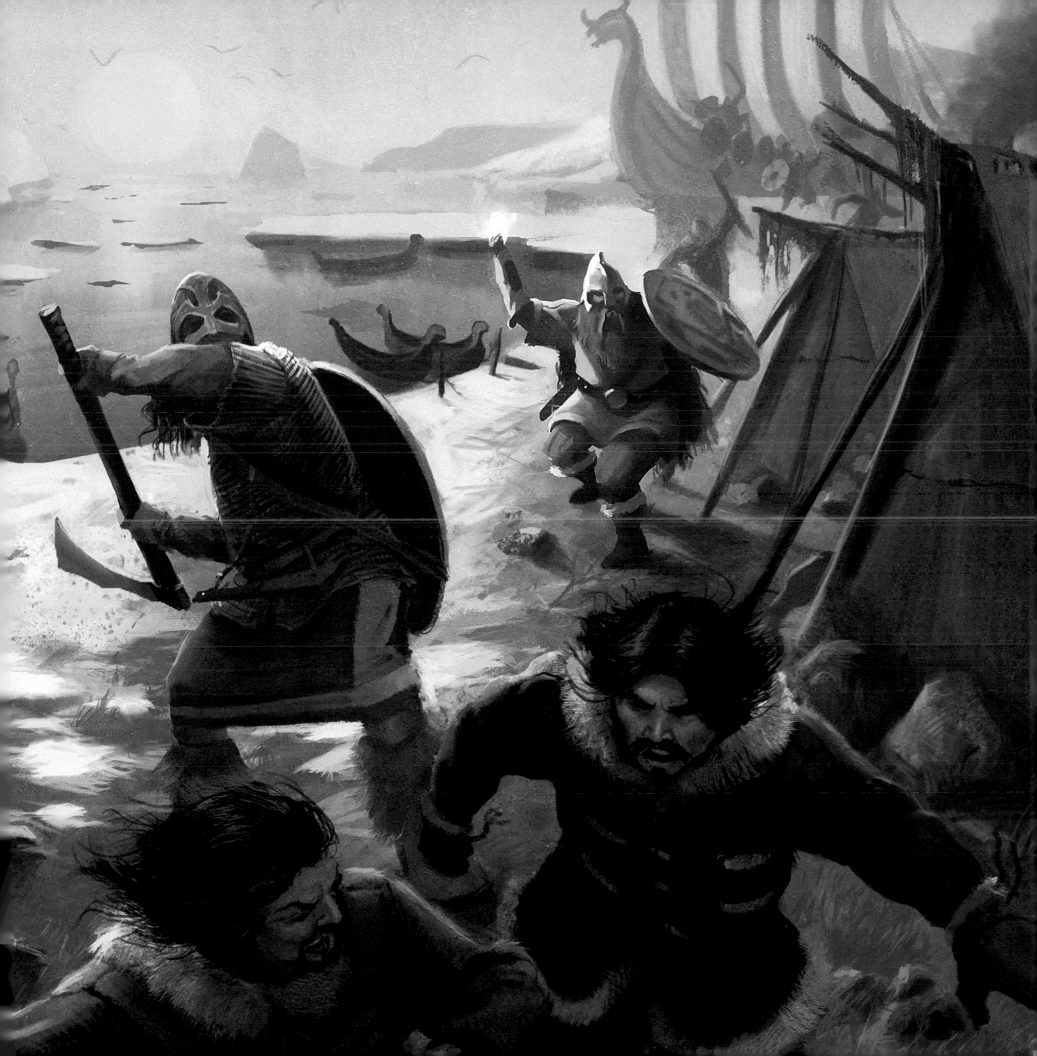

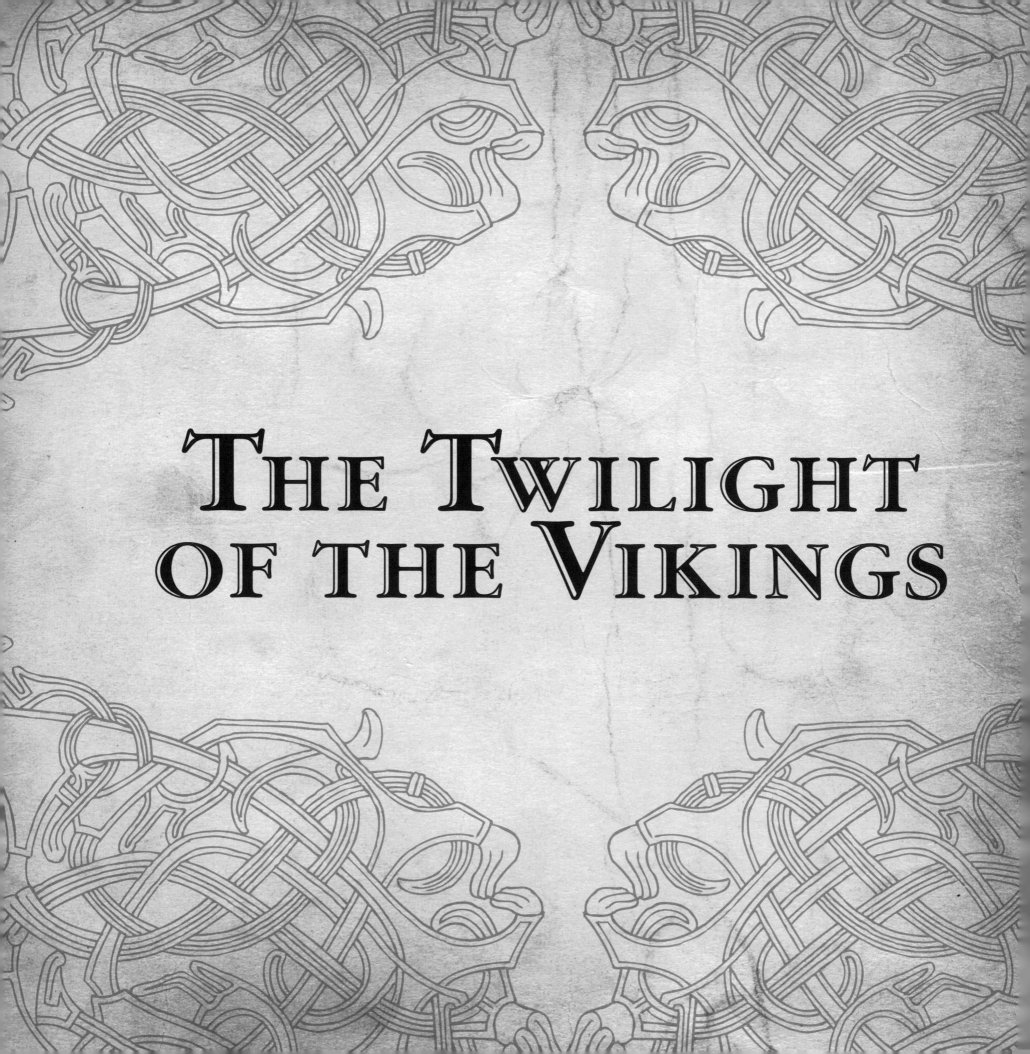

The Twilight
of the Vikings

❧ THE END OF GREENLAND ❧

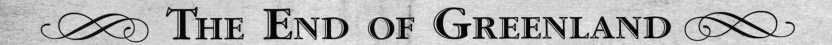

Greenland remained a remote outpost of the Viking world, and with little to trade, there was little incentive for many European merchant ships to make the long and dangerous voyage to visit. This became particularly difficult in the later Middle Ages, as a cooling in the general climate caused pack ice to drift further south every year, creating new shipping hazards. With months, sometimes years, going past without contact with Greenland, some in Europe speculated that the colony had been abandoned.

There is some evidence that the Greenlanders always knew they were not alone—scattered debris near their settlements suggested there were earlier visitors. During the twelfth century, these visitors began to return, and the Greenlanders had to compete with the returning Inuit (Thule Eskimos) over their northern hunting grounds.

Both Icelandic sagas and ancient Eskimo legends mention battles between the Eskimos and Europeans. The Eskimos called them the Kavdlunait ("Foreigners"), and although there were sporadic attempts to trade, the relationship became increasingly desperate as Greenland grew colder.

121

What Happened to the Greenlanders?

Eventually, there was no more word from the Greenland colony, and a visiting ship in the fifteenth century found the place deserted, with a single dead body lying where it had fallen. Legends, unsupported by genetic profiling, suggest that some of the settlers joined the Eskimos. Others, equally without evidence, say that the Greenlanders sailed away, though if they aimed for Iceland, there is no record of them ever arriving. Since there were no dead bodies save the one, it seems unlikely that they all died of plague. It could be that the last of the Greenlanders cannot be found because, with food in increasingly short supply, they were eaten. The most likely explanation, however, is that they were carried off by English pirates, and sold as slaves in the Muslim world.

Lords Of The Isles

While Vikings faded away in Greenland, turned to farming in Iceland, went native in England and became civilized locals in their native Scandinavia, the Viking spirit continued to endure in some outlying areas. In particular, the geography and isolation of the remote Scottish isles encouraged local men to hang onto old skills. Communication required boats by necessity, and ownership of boats led men to be fishermen in times of peace, and to settle disputes in time of strife by raiding neighboring islands.

Cull Of Kintyre

More than a hundred years after the official end of the Viking age, Norse descendants continued to fight over power and wealth in Scotland. A man by the name of Somerled is recorded as the king of Kintyre in 1140, when he married the daughter of Amlaith (Olaf), the king of the Isle of Man. Although little is known about Somerled's origins or power, he was enough of an old-school Viking to seize his chances in 1153 when both his father-in-law on Man and King David of Scotland died. But Somerled's war was not a straight-forward land-grab like that of Harald Fairhair. Instead, he clung at least in part to the idea of a legitimate succession, claiming that his wife's brother was unfit to rule Man, and that instead his own son Dougal, grandson of the late king, was a far better choice as King of the Isles.

122

Somerled fought his brother-in-law to a standstill with a fleet of 80 ships in 1156, forcing him to first split the area with him, and then, two years later, to give it all to him. His rival fled to safety in Norway, and Somerled became the undisputed ruler of the entire north-west coast of Scotland, and the islands off its shores, until 1164, when he died in suspicious circumstance, probably in battle with the Stewart kings of Scotland.

Norse descendants continued to fight over power and wealth in Scotland

Foreigner Gaelic

Somerled's rule demonstrated just how integrated the Scots and the Scandinavians had become, creating a hybrid race known locally as the Gall-Gaidheal or "Foreigner-Gaelic." Modern genetic studies have suggested that Somerled has over half a million living descendants—almost as many as Genghis Khan.

Viking Names In Scotland

Many Scottish names retain the suggestions of Viking ancestry, particularly once we strip away the "Mac" that means "son of":

MacAskill	*Son of Asketill*
MacAuliffe	*Son of Olaf*
MacIver	*Son of Ivar/Ingvar*
MacKitrick	*Son of Sigtrygg*
MacLeod	*Son of Ljot (literally 'Son of Ugly')*
MacSweeney	*Son of Svein*
McCorkindale	*Son of Thorketill*

Svein's Spring Breaks

Svein Asleifarson, based in the Orkney islands, was another such Viking-age throwback, flourishing around the same time as Somerled. But Svein lacked any pretence of royal power, instead living an old-fashioned life of farming and fishing, with a band of perhaps eighty warriors. He first turned to raiding in the 1130s when he was briefly outlawed for his part in a family feud. It was Svein's habit to head off on two raiding trips a year, one in the spring after sowing his crops, and another in the autumn once the harvest had been collected. As his reputation grew, he became popular with local barons as a "hit man," and rented out his services for tailor-made raids on his clients' enemies. He made it to a ripe old age for a Viking, but died fighting in 1171 in the aftermath to recapture the Irish town of Dublin from Anglo-Norman invaders.

The Northern Crusades

The Vikings were first defined as and feared for being pagan pirates who were prepared to attack Christian sites. With the end of the Viking age and the conversion to Christianity, Scandinavian aggression was directed away from the Christian world, and hence was no longer regarded as so noteworthy by European chroniclers. Raids and conflicts in the Viking style continued on the eastern shores of the Baltic Sea, except this time they were often conducted in the name of Jesus Christ.

The people on the Swedish coast were less worried about pagans than about would-be Vikings. They suffered regular sea-borne attacks from the east, including Karelian Finns, Osilian Estonians, and Curonians. These groups followed the old Viking habits of seasonal plundering, but the raiding parties were often quite small and not deemed worth a full-scale Swedish retaliation. When local funds ran low, however, the Swedes were apt to find religion. In 1142, a fleet of sixty Swedish ships committed acts of piracy on the Baltic Sea against merchants returning from the east. A Russian chronicle recorded that the raiders were led by "a prince of the Swedes and a bishop," suggesting that, on paper at least, the old type of Viking raid now enjoyed the support of the royal family and the church.

Although some of the attacks were referred to as "crusades" in contemporary accounts, others were originally regarded as much more old-fashioned wars or raids, and only renamed Crusades in the ninetenth century, as part of a movement to present the Swedish nation as devout, and the conquest of the eastern territories as a pious act.

King Eric IX of Sweden led a large-scale military assault on Finland in the 1150s, which was later called the "first Finland Crusade"—its purpose one of conquering Finnish territory (which would remain part of Sweden for several centuries) and also converting the inhabitants to Christianity.

Scandinavian aggression was directed away from the Christian world

Prince Eric, brother of the Norwegian King Sverrir, "went into the Baltic to plunder heathen lands" in 1186—a typical Viking raid, with only the word "heathen" added to his justification for stealing from the Finns and Estonians.

In 1193, Pope Celestine III called for a proper "crusade" in northeast Europe to bring the heathen peoples of what is now Poland, Estonia and Finland into the Christian faith. There may have been other issues behind the scenes—parts of the area to be "saved" included territories that already had resident missionaries from the Orthodox Russian church. At least some of the "heathens" attacked in Celestine's crusades were already Christians, albeit not of the sort of Christianity that Celestine himself followed.

In 1219 Danish crusaders established their rule over the south coast of the Gulf of Finland. Their base had a church dedicated to Saint Olaf, and became known in the local language as either Talv-linna ("Winter Fort") or Taani-linna ("Fort of the Danes"). It is now known as Tallinn, and is the capital of modern Estonia.

125

THE KENSINGTON STONE AND OTHER MYSTERIES

Nobody doubts that Norse explorers visited America, although just when and where remains a hot topic. A genuine Viking-era coin from the era of Magnus the Good was found in Maine, although that in itself is not proof that it was left there by Vikings. It could just as easily have made its way from further north in the hands of Native American owners after being traded for or found near Leif's Booths.

The Kensington Stone was found entangled in the roots of a tree on farmland being cleared in Minnesota in September 1898. It was carved with strange runes that appeared to describe a lost Viking expedition deep into America, perhaps through the Great Lakes or Hudson Bay. The find caused great excitement, particularly among America's Scandinavian immigrant community, as it implied much more extensive contacts with Vinland than had previously been noted.

126

However, the stone is widely thought to be a fake. Some of the runes were regarded as anachronisms, although the stone's defenders have pointed out that no Viking had a dictionary so errors could arise, and modern linguists are not sure what words were used in different dialects. The stone was originally found at the time of the Chicago World's Fair in 1893, when immigrant pride was swelled by the arrival of a replica Viking ship and the approaching 900th anniversary of Leif's discovery of Vinland. Could it have been an elaborate hoax?

Bacterial Invaders?

Archaeological evidence in America suggests that the continent may have suffered from an outbreak of tuberculosis around A.D. 1000. Although the outbreak may have had another source, it probably came from Native American contact with Europeans. Signs of the disease eventually spread as far south as Peru. Could it initially have been picked up from unmentioned Viking explorations far into the American heartland?

There are other tantalizing bits of Viking evidence scattered across North America. Several runic inscriptions have been found in the modern age, although it has not yet been possible to verify their origins. A stone in Heavener, Oklahoma, is carved with markings that might read "Glomedal"—"Glome's valley" in runes. Another, in nearby Shawnee, reads "Medok"—possibly a name. Another collection of stones in Spirit Pond, Maine, includes a long runic inscription telling of a Viking shipwreck. But were they left there by Norse explorers or put there by local hoaxers?

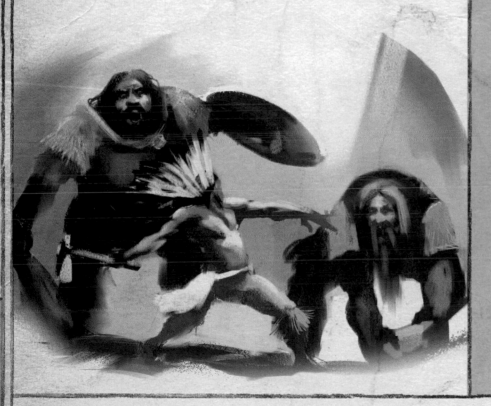

Red Horn and the Giants

Southwest Wisconsin's Gottschall Rock Shelter is a cave in a ravine that was inhabited by Ho-Chunk (Winnebago) Indians for many centuries. Radiocarbon dating has established that a particular mural was drawn on its wall between A.D. 900 and 1100, depicting a local hero called Red Horn fighting two red-haired giants. Local legend told of a red-haired woman whose followers challenged the Ho-Chunk to a sporting contest, which devolved into a brawl. The red-haired woman later became Red Horn's wife.

127

Are these stories and fragments the last remaining evidence of more European explorers in medieval America, and perhaps even the final destination of the lost Greenland colony?

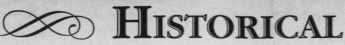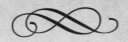

In 1354, King Magnus Erikson of Sweden and Norway ordered an expedition to be led by Norwegian Paul Knutson on a voyage to Greenland. The Western Settlement of Greenland had been found abandoned a few years earlier and it was believed the population had reverted to their old pagan way and left for what is now North America. The importance of the mission is shown by the fact that Knutson was allowed to use the Royal Knorr (a type of boat) and to choose his companions from the King's corps of bodyguards.

In 1577, a letter from Gerardus Mercator, a Flemish cartographer, to John Dee, philosopher to Queen Elizabeth of England, excerpts an earlier work by Jacobus Cnoyen that described a voyage into the Arctic that returned in 1364 with eight survivors. Knutson was not among the survivors. The voyage was apparently accompanied by a priest who documented the voyage, and its route, in a book called the *Inventio Fortunate*. Although no copy of this book has ever been found it is mentioned in many documents from the period.

INVENTIO FORTUNATE

This mysterious book was apparently used by sixteenth century cartographers as the source for their information about the Arctic region. Some maps even show Hudson Bay over 100 years before Henry Hudson's "discovery." It is said that the book and the subsequent maps influenced Columbus's plans to sail across the Atlantic.

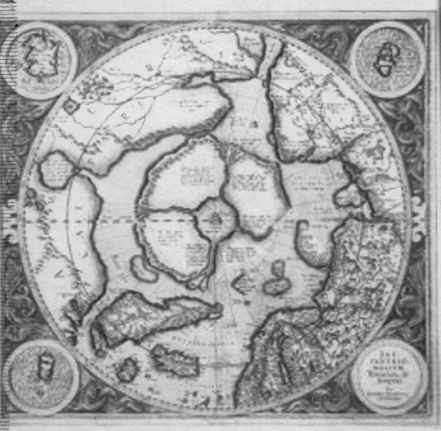

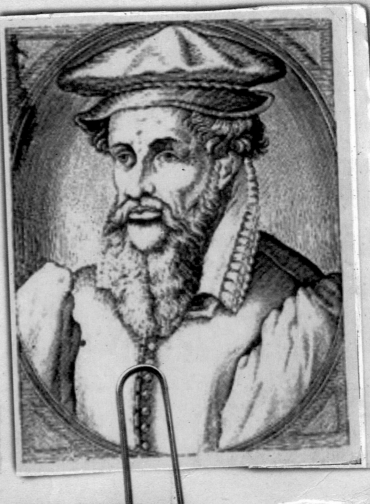

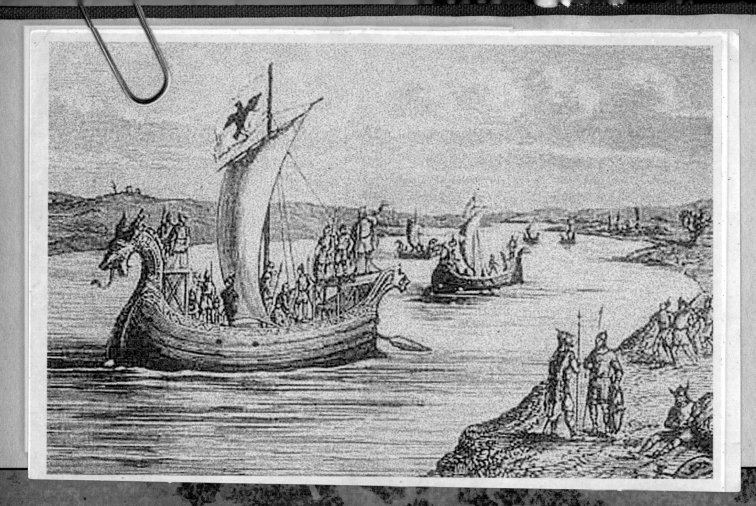

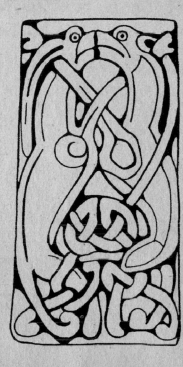

Western Colony

Eastern Colony

Possible Route Through
St. Lawrence River

Possible Route Following
Vinland Exploration Routes

Kensington

Vinland

Greenland
to Minnesota

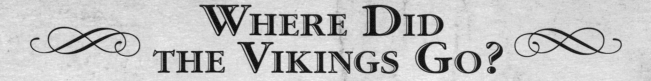

WHERE DID THE VIKINGS GO?

The Vikings disappear from history soon after 1066, but where did they go? Approximately 200,000 young men left Scandinavia during the Viking Age to form the criminal element of Viking raiders that caused much trouble for the Christian world. But with many now dead in battle or transformed into settlers, the end of the Viking Age had arrived.

Vikings had settled all over the regions they had once terrorized—usually with local wives, whose children would grow up speaking the local language. Within a couple of generations, most children of the Vikings identified themselves as English, Normans, or Russians, but not as Vikings.

The Vikings were first feared because they had been prepared to attack Christian targets. Now that they were, at least nominally, Christians, they were no longer feared by the church. Instead, they often worked for it. Many warriors who might have once been Vikings were transformed into crusaders, channeling their aggression away from Christendom and against its enemies. Some Scandinavians became "Jerusalem-farers," fighting in the Holy Land, but many more took part in the Baltic Crusades, military operations against areas of what is now Poland, Latvia, and Lithuania.

As for the Viking leaders of the Middle Ages, their descendants still exist today. Genetic surveys have found heavy concentrations of Norwegian genes in the north of England, Scotland, and the Scottish islands. The royal families of Europe, including the rulers of England and Norway, continue to count the likes of Harald the Ruthless and Olaf the Stout among their ancestors.

128

Maeshowe

The ancient grave-mound of Maeshowe in the Orkney Islands was known as Orkshowe in the Middle Ages. It bears several scraps of Viking graffiti in its interior grave chamber, mainly regarding the looks and attitudes of local girls. The place seems to have been a favored spot for secret trysts. Right above the door is a faded carving: That er vikingr . . . kom undir her til—"It is a Viking . . . came under to this place." *However, the Viking's name is now missing. Another rune carving shows that even though they were no longer Vikings, Scandinavian crusaders were still keen to make their mark.*

The Varangians' Last Stand

In Byzantium, the Varangian Guard was a popular destination for Viking fortune seekers for several hundred years, but began to lose its exclusively Scandinavian character in the eleventh century. After the Norman conquest of England in 1066, many English warriors sought employment with the Byzantine army, and the Varangians lost their Viking character. The last battle of the Varangians was fought in 1204, when they reluctantly and unsuccessfully defended Constantinople against attacking Crusaders.

Return to Vinland

By the late nineteenth century, a new group of emigrants was leaving Scandinavia for the New World, and many of them settled in the northern United States, amid lands and vistas that reminded them of home. The lakes and forests of Minnesota, in particular, appealed to many of Swedish or Norwegian origin. Toward the end of the nineteenth century, when Vikings became popular figures in modern literature, the disparate Scandinavians of the region began to develop a sense of pride, not in being the descendants of various Norwegians, Swedes, Danes, and Finns, but in being united by a connection to Vikings.

The Viking Spirit

But for those who believe that there was more to the medieval Scandinavian achievement than mere raids and murders, the old spirit of exploration has not died. The furthest point from the "old world," the Bering Strait between Alaska and Siberia, bears the name of a Danish-Swedish explorer, Vitus Bering. And far above the seas the Vikings once sailed, Aldrin Crater on the Moon bears the Swedish surname of the pilot of the Eagle lander, Edwin "Buzz" Aldrin.

129

✠ TIMELINE ✠

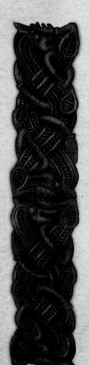

c.737	Construction begins on the Danevirke
789	Scandinavian sailors murder a local sheriff in southern Britain
792	King Offa of Mercia constructs fortifications on the eastern coast of Britain
793	Viking attack on Lindisfarne
800	Approximate date of the Oseberg ship burial
815	Death of Charlemagne causes strife in the Frankish empire
c.825	First Scandinavian converts to Christianity
840	Viking settlers at the "black pool" (Dubh-linn) in Ireland
843	Viking attack on Nantes
c.860	Gardar is blown off course and discovers Iceland
859	Hastein and Bjorn Ironside attack the Mediterranean coast
860	Weland is paid by Charles the Bald to defend France from other Vikings
862	Foundation of the Viking town of Novgorod in Russia
867	Foundation of the Viking kingdom of York in northern Britain
870	Completion of the Ponte de l'Arche fortified bridge
870-930	Colonization of Iceland
871	Alfred the Great crowned king of Wessex; attacks by Guthrum and the Great Heathen Host
872	Harald Fairhair becomes first true king of Norway
878	Defeat of Guthrum by Alfred; Guthrum is baptized as part of the treaty agreement
886	Alfred the Great allows the Vikings to establish the Danelaw in eastern Britain; occupies London to ensure control of the River Thames into Wessex
c.900	Gokstad ship burial
911	Foundation of the Viking duchy of Normandy in northern France
912	Viking sailors first carry their ships across the gap from the River Don to the River Volga, enabling them to reach Arab trading posts on the Caspian Sea
922	Ibn Fadlan writes an account of Vikings on the Caspian Sea coast
936	Erik the Red reaches Greenland

130

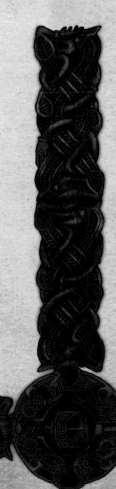

c.943	*Decline of Muslim market for slaves from Scandinavian traders; focus of Viking activity shifts back to Britain and Europe*
c.970	*Poppo the priest supposedly impresses King Harald Bluetooth with the power of Christian belief; Harald eventually converts to Christianity*
988	*Foundation of the Varangian Guard in Byzantium; it attracts Viking mercenaries for the next hundred years*
991	*King Athelred II "the Unready" is forced to bribe Danish raiders to keep them away from England; the first payment of danegeld*
1000	*Iceland accepts Christianity; Leif Erikson explores coast of Vinland*
1002	*The Saint Brice's Day massacre, in which the English attempt to kill all Danish immigrants*
1003	*Svein Forkbeard attacks England*
1013	*Svein Forkbeard proclaims himself King of England, but dies soon after*
1016	*Svein Forkbeard's son, Canute, becomes King of England*
c.1020	*Vinland colony is abandoned*
1028	*Canute conquers Norway*
1030	*Olaf the Stout (later Saint Olaf) is killed at the Battle of Stiklistad; his teenage brother Harald the Ruthless goes into exile, serving as a mercenary in Russia, then Byzantium*
1066	*Harald the Ruthless makes a claim on the throne of England, but is defeated at the battle of Stamford Bridge; the victorious army is too weak to resist a second invasion in the south by William "the Conqueror"*
1096-1099	*First Crusade; many Scandinavian men who might have become Vikings instead become "Jerusalem-farers" and fight in the Holy Land*
1147	*First Northern Crusade on the coasts of the Baltic Sea*
1241	*Death of Snorri Sturluson*
1347	*Last recorded trip by Greenlanders to Canada, in search of timber*

131

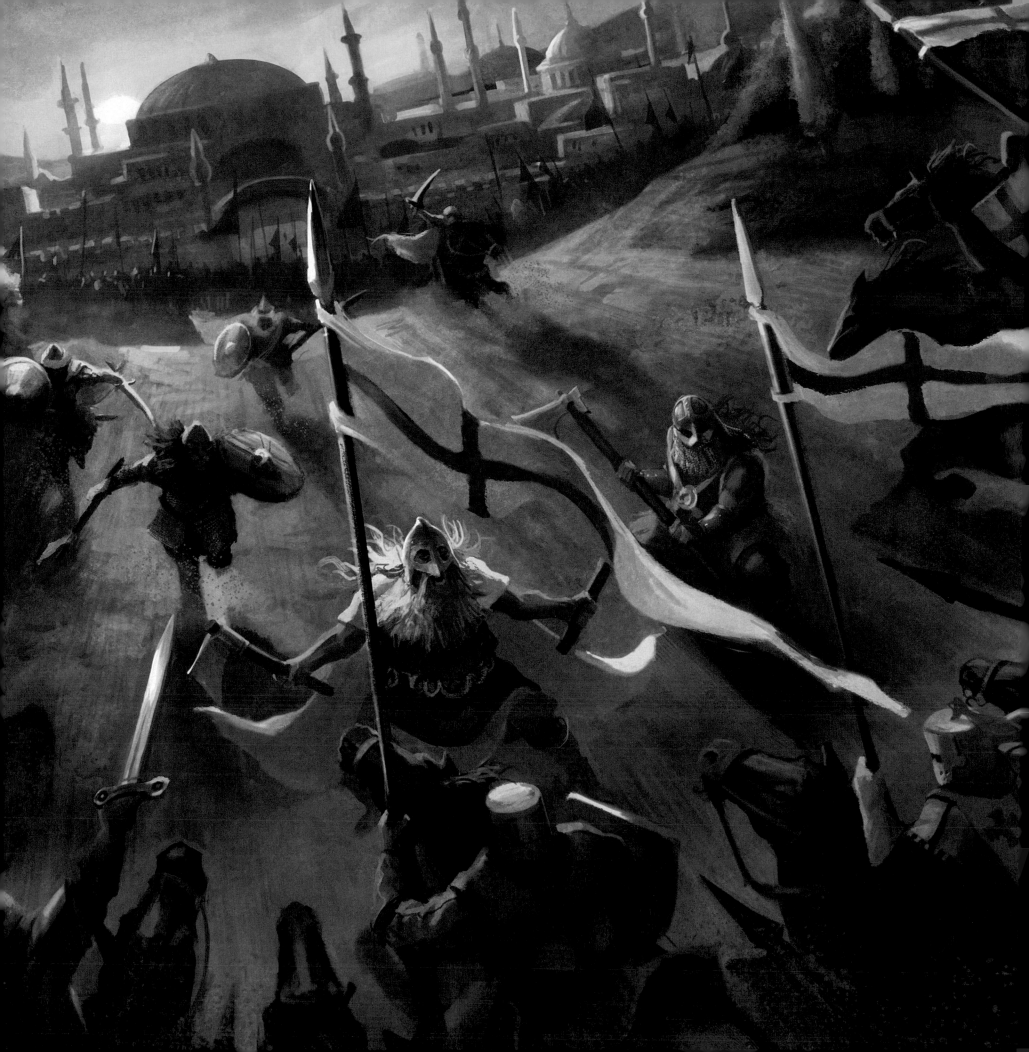

INDEX

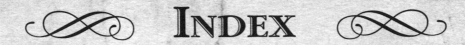

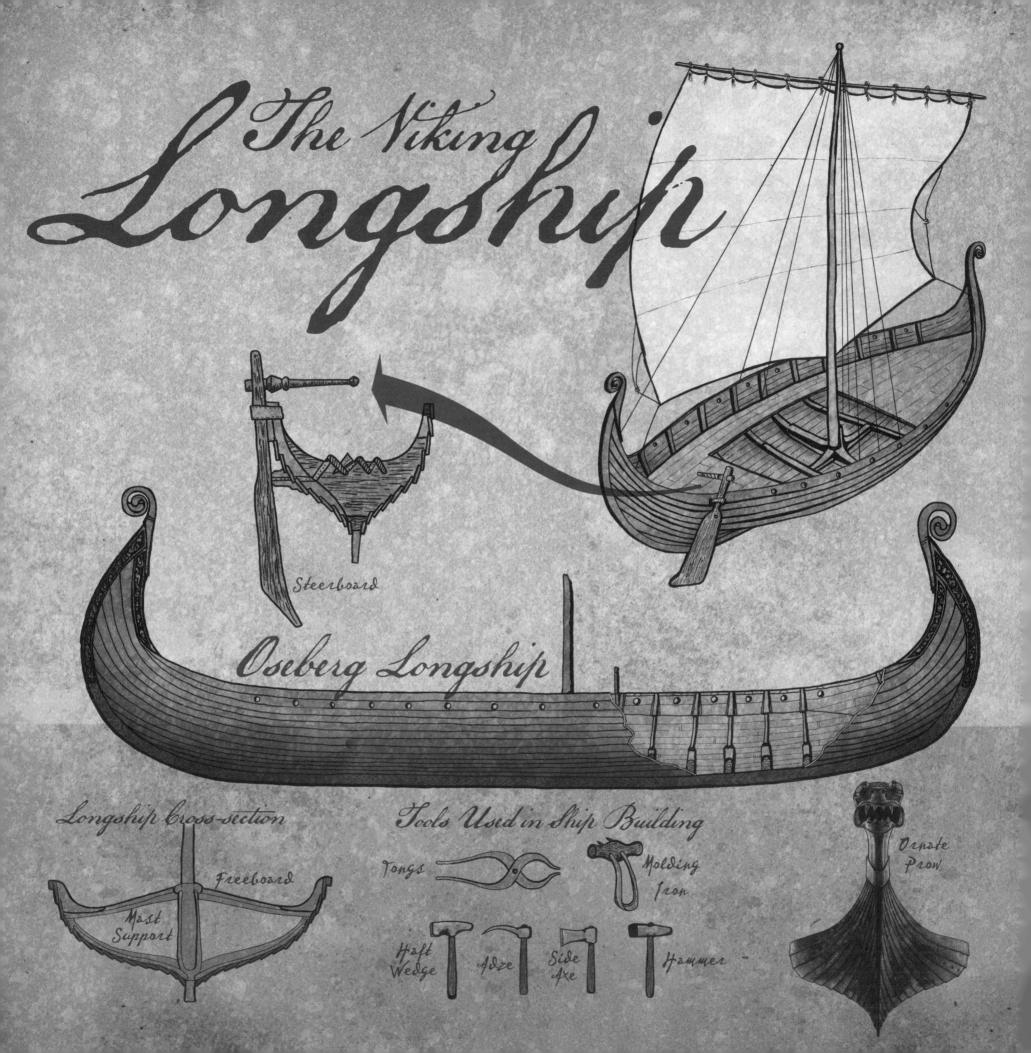

The Viking Longship

Steerboard

Oseberg Longship

Longship Cross-section

Freeboard

Mast Support

Tools Used in Ship Building

Tongs

Molding Iron

Haft Wedge

Adze

Side Axe

Hammer

Ornate Prow